Leading Into the World

Other Books in the Vital Worship, Healthy Congregations Series

Leading Into the World

Paul Galbreath

ROWMAN & LITTLEFIELD
Lanham • Boulder • New York • London

Published by Rowman & Littlefield
A wholly owned subsidiary of The Rowman & Littlefield Publishing Group, Inc.
4501 Forbes Boulevard, Suite 200, Lanham, Maryland 20706
www.rowman.com

16 Carlisle Street, London W1D 3BT, United Kingdom

British Library Cataloguing in Publication Information Available

Library of Congress Cataloging-in-Publication Data

Galbreath, Paul, author.
Leading into the world / Paul Galbreath.
p. cm.
Includes bibliographical references.
ISBN 978-1-56699-760-7 (cloth : alk. paper) -- ISBN 978-1-56699-719-5 (pbk. : alk. paper) -- ISBN 978-1-56699-720-1 (electronic)
1. Nature--Religious aspects--Christianity. 2. Human ecology--Religious aspects--Christianity. 3. Christian stewardship. 4. Worship programs. 5. Church year. I. Title.
BR115.N3G35 2014
261.8'8--dc23

2014026960

Printed in the United States of America

For Marisa Mangum and Ben Paroulek,
in thanksgiving for long and rich friendships

Contents

Acknowledgments

I am particularly grateful to The Louisville Institute for a generous research grant that allowed me to explore these themes on my sabbatical. During the year that I lived in the Pacific Northwest, I worshipped, preached, taught, and met regularly with six Presbyterian congregations in Oregon, Washington, and British Columbia: Valley Community in Portland; First Newport; Pioneer in Warrenton; St. Andrew's in Victoria, British Columbia; Church of the Indian Fellowship in Tacoma; and First Cambodian in Tacoma. I am grateful for their openness, engagement, and input that helped shape my initial work on this topic. My own institution, Union Presbyterian Seminary, provided a sabbatical that allowed me to work on this project. In addition, Charles Freeman and Shardé Chapman worked with me as students in a class on Ecology and Worship and helped me think through many of the topics in this book.

I am especially grateful to Danny Colnon and Marisa Mangum, who opened their home to me and gave me a place to write the first draft of this manuscript, as well as offering encouragement along the way. This book is dedicated to two long-term friends who bring me great joy and who have given me much support through both good and hard times. Thank you, Ben and Marisa! My super editor, Beth Gaede, provided me with great questions and suggestions.

Thanks as well to my wife, Jan, who supported this project every step of the way and whose connections to the earth run much deeper than mine. For our son, Andi, who is a gift and blessing in our lives, this book offers reflections on ways that those of us in church can learn to speak and act to preserve the earth for future generations. I offer this book in the hope that it will encourage and prod us to find ways to more closely connect our faith with our care of this good earth.

Preface

How does Christian faith, formed and nurtured in worship, connect with our acts of caring for the earth? That is the question that lies at the center of this book. This is the third in a series of books on sacramental ethics, language I use to explore how worship and the sacraments relate to our daily lives. I did not set out to write a trilogy. However, along the way, my questions grew about the connections between our words and actions in the sanctuary and the choices that we make each day. I started by exploring the shape of our prayer at the communion table in *Leading from the Table* before turning to observe the dimensions of baptismal life in *Leading through the Water*.[1]

This volume builds on the groundwork from the earlier books by reflecting on how the earth as God's good gift provides us with places and resources for worship. My awareness of the significance of creation care as a central part of Christian discipleship is in itself an act of faith in God the creator of heaven and earth. In this time of environmental crises and climate change, Christians are called to reexamine our language and priorities in order to make necessary changes to preserve life on this fragile planet. By life, I am thinking about much more than human lives or even plants and animals. As readers will see, these are reflections on this vast, interconnected ecosystem in which we live.

This book explores how our actions of earth-care can be grounded in our prayers and liturgies. Following each chapter, the reader will find a set of worship resources for a particular season of the liturgical year—from Advent to ordinary time. The liturgical year itself has its roots in the harvest festivals of early Judaism. The early church built on these foundations by associating Christian observances with Jewish festivals. For example, historical and theological correlations provided connections between the memories of Jesus's death and resurrection and the celebration of Passover.[2] The first Christian communities preserved the Jewish roots of many holidays while expanding them to serve their own theological priorities among rapidly increasing Gentile Christian communities.

The decision to celebrate the birth of Christ at the time of the winter solstice provided Christian communities a way to mark time in their religious gatherings that traced the seasons of the year. The Roman festival celebrating the return of light as the days begin to get longer was given Christological significance by connecting the birth of the Christ child to this celebration. The story of Christ's birth interpreted as the light that comes into the world found a natural correlation with the celebration of the winter solstice and the longer days of sunlight. Over time, the church extended these connections by adding the celebration of Epiphany as the manifestation of the light, and the celebration of Jesus's baptism as an event that brought God's blessing to all creation. Augustine and other early church fathers described Jesus's entrance into the Jordan River to be baptized by John as an act that made all water sacred. Through his baptism and time of temptation and discernment in the wilderness, Jesus modeled a call to ministry and service. The early church developed the season of Lent to provide a time of preparation for those who would be baptized as part of the Easter celebrations.[3]

The Book of Acts links the history of the church and the coming of the Holy Spirit with the celebration of Pentecost by many who gathered in Jerusalem shortly after Jesus's death and resurrection. Here, the confluence of a spring harvest festival and the memory and proclamation of Jesus's life led to an ecstatic experience, providing the initial impetus for Jewish Christians to form a close-knit community marked by care for one another and the regular breaking of bread (both presented as signs of Eucharistic life). The church year moves from the memory of this founding to an extended period of ordinary time, one of sharing in daily life and activities that lead to a mature faith. Ordinary time follows the rhythms of the earth and emphasizes seasonal growth.

The worship materials in this book consist of two related resources: service prayers and liturgical material, and a Eucharistic prayer for each of the seasons of the church year. The prayers include a call to worship, confession and pardon, prayer for illumination, prayer of dedication, and prayer of the day (known as a *collect* in some traditions). Charles Freeman wrote prayers of the day for each season in my class on Ecology and Worship. I have adapted his work so that it coordinates with the other worship resources in the book. While different traditions place these elements in various parts of the service, the primary purpose of the material is to show ways that these seasonal prayers can consistently include the earth in our worship. Similarly, the Eucharistic prayers that are provided highlight aspects of each particular season while including images of the earth as a regular part of our table prayers.

One important note is that each of the Eucharistic prayers draws on a particular meal narrative from the Gospels or the Book of Acts. Recent research on the development of Eucharistic prayers shows the significance of the meal tradition throughout the Gospels, from the feeding of the 5,000 to the multiple narratives of Jesus's eating with diverse groups of people, to the resurrection stories that include meals (e.g., Emmaus in Luke 22 and John 21). Each Eucharistic prayer focuses on one of these meals as a way of expanding the church's vision beyond its primary focus on the Last Supper (much more on this in chapter 3). While the texts of the Eucharistic prayers provided here do not include the words of institution, their traditional place in the order of a communion prayer is marked with asterisks so that presiders can include them in the body of the prayer if they choose to do so.[4]

Chapter One

Reconnecting to the Earth

Ten years ago, my wife, Jan, and I went to Greece. On a sunny, spring morning, we wandered around the ruins of Delphi. It was one of those magical days where we had the ancient, sacred place virtually to ourselves. That afternoon, filled with awe, we began driving across the Greek peninsula to explore the ancient monasteries of Meteora. The tree-lined highway across the flat plains was surrounded by rich farmland. As I drove, we began to notice that some of the trees were dying. At first, it was a topic of conversation between the two of us as we wondered what had caused the infestation. But as we went further, the tragedy subdued us. For mile after mile, we drove past rows of dying trees. Our conversation ceased and we simply wept as we saw the earth dying around us. When we asked people in the region what happened to the trees, we were told that the pollution from trucks using leaded gas poisoned the air and led to their death.

This experience of seeing and feeling the scars of the earth was a wake-up call for me. No longer could I turn my back on the earth's pain and pretend that I did not contribute to it. It was time to take stock of the ways that my life contributed to the pollution and destruction of the environment. As one who professed faith in "God the Father, almighty, maker of heaven and earth," I faced the question: How was I caring for this earth? Or to go deeper: In what ways does my faith demonstrate my gratitude for the gift of this good earth? As we will see, the creation stories in Genesis present a compelling portrait of the interrelatedness of our world. Humans, plants, animals, water, rocks—all of creation is presented as the work of God.

These questions about how gratitude leads to Christian responsibility to care for the earth stand at the center of this book. In particular, I am interested in exploring how our Sunday gathering to worship God prompts us to engage in acts of kindness toward one another and all creation. Many people find worship shapes us and provides patterns of faith in our daily lives.

Whether we consider the role of worship in terms of cultivating patterns and virtues, or learning values through Scripture and communal practices, the church teaches us to see and experience the world around us in particular ways.[1] Through our participation, we learn to practice hospitality, serve others, and become involved in the life of the community. At times in the church's history, congregations have provided significant contrasts to the prevailing patterns and beliefs of dominant cultures. Consider congregations that worked to end slavery in the nineteenth century or, more recently, churches that have provided sanctuary to undocumented workers. Less dramatically, my own congregation practices hospitality each week by welcoming members from the adult home down the street to fully participate in the life of the community.

Even so, it is important to notice the ways that churches may also fail to school us in practices that challenge the dominant values of the surrounding culture. For example, how many of our congregations consider actions that stand in contrast to the dominant cultural patterns of consumption and greed? When we take our youth to theme parks or the mall, how are we teaching them about the Gospel's call to care for the poor and marginalized? What cultural values does a congregation's Sunday celebration of national holidays or its placement of the American flag at the front of the sanctuary reinforce?[2] How often do we talk about money from a faith perspective? For example, does investing a congregation's endowment in stocks and bonds support a capitalist philosophy of the marketplace?

Stepping back to critically examine our assumptions and practices provides an important opportunity to take inventory of the ways that our language and practices in worship teach us to see and live in the world.[3] In times of challenge, crisis, and change, taking inventory allows us to look at our own patterns and practices that contribute to the plight we are facing.

When I experienced a sense of profound loss and grief with the death of trees on the plains of Greece, I found myself asking questions about what worship has taught me regarding gratitude for creation and my responsibility to care for the earth. What are we communicating in our liturgies? When we gather in our sanctuaries, in what ways do we identify and relate to the needs of the earth? How does liturgy shape our imagination to live in ways that support the earth's needs?

TAKING AN INVENTORY

When we turn our attention to the relationship of the earth to our Sunday morning services, we usually experience an immediate sense of disconnection. For most of us, the earth rarely shows up in our worship services. We might mention a recent natural disaster during the prayers of the people or offer a prayer for rain in a time of drought. Otherwise, images of the earth are strangely absent. Barricaded inside our sanctuaries, where stained glass windows prevent us from seeing the world outside, we are left with only bouquets of cut flowers as reminders of creation. Our language in worship reinforces the drastic sense of separation we have created: we leave the sanctuary to go back to the routines of our daily lives. Even the language of sending at the end of the service reinforces this division. We are sent out into the world as if we had gathered in a place cut off from it, as if our churches exist in a space apart from the world itself.

A myriad of complex reasons led Christians to separate themselves from the world, particularly their natural environment. Since the earliest years of the church, Christians have been challenged by Gnosticism, a belief that true knowledge of salvation allows one to escape the confines of this world and that spiritual truths should not be tainted by the material world. Some early Gnostics went so far as to declare that Jesus only appeared to be human, since divinity would be contaminated by physical nature or the matter of the earth. While the church eventually condemned Gnosticism as a heresy, its influence has remained pervasive. We encounter it in the tendency to see the earth more as a fallen place than as the arena of God's glory.

Another factor that widened the divide between the church and the world was the growing withdrawal of clergy and monks into monasteries or other lives apart from the normal lives of baptized Christians. With this move, the church reinforced the tendency to see spiritual work as belonging to only certain leaders. Church members engaged in their daily tasks and then came to church in order to gain the benefits and insights that only these leaders could provide. This separation between the realm of the sacred and secular prompted many to think of faith as related only to the activities of the church. While broader notions of vocation identified individuals' daily work as their calling, in many circles only those at the top of an imagined church hierarchy were thought to be called—to have vocations. One might speak of one's calling as a farmer or craftsman or parent, but the calling to ordained ministry was viewed as a preferred vocation, because it dealt with spiritual matters rather than physical or everyday work.

Over time, further theological arguments were built on this scaffolding. Some Protestants, especially those within the Reformed tradition, inherited a theology in which God's revelation is narrowly defined solely in terms of Jesus Christ. In some circles, this view has led to a reluctance to speak of God's presence in any part of creation. Even the elements of the sacraments (water, bread, and wine) are suspect. From this perspective, a prayer that blesses these gifts—that invites us to see and experience the presence of Christ in the water in this font, or the bread and wine on this table—is considered heretical. From this perspective, God's revelation is confined to Scripture's witness to Jesus Christ. Once again, we are understood as isolated from the world, and salvation becomes a spiritual escape from this fallen planet.

An inability or unwillingness to see the world as a sacred gift in need of care prompted European settlers coming to the United States to claim manifest destiny, the conviction that God gave the land to them to conquer and subdue. The earth and the forces of nature were understood as hostile elements to be brought under human control. Harnessing the resources of the earth to support human productivity became a primary goal of the movement westward across the North American continent.

Particular interpretations of Scripture kept humans apart from the rest of creation. Note particularly the standard interpretation of the creation story in Genesis, where humans were given "dominion" over the earth. Here any notion of stewardship or shared responsibility was overwhelmed by what Christians understood as the divine command to subjugate and conquer the earth. Theologian Belden Lane describes this theological shift among the Puritans who moved from a sense of delight about the abundance of the land that "echoes the divine image" to an "unrestrained use of creation as 'serviceable goods' satisfying the needs of an expanding economy."[4]

Recent critiques of this interpretation of *dominion* focus on the way in which humans place themselves at the center of the world, with the earth as ours to conquer and subdue or to use in whatever way we see fit. In contrast, recent scholarship understands the creation narratives in Genesis as underscoring the interrelationship among all forms of life and human responsibility to care for and tend the earth. While this shift in interpretations is ongoing in many congregations, it is important to note how even the language promoting human stewardship of the earth often maintains a sense of hierarchy, with humans at the top of the chain maintaining the power to determine the fate of other forms of life.

In our lifetime, Christian faith is increasingly defined as a private matter, between each of us and God. Individuals are left to work this out on their own in the privacy of their homes. The influence of the market-driven economy popularizes the notion that spirituality is a product to be marketed to individual consumers. Spirituality has become a matter of personal growth. In this approach, faith supports individual accomplishment. Once again, such a narrow form of spirituality largely removes us from our relationship to and responsibility for the world around us.

Accompanying this emphasis on individual spirituality, popular definitions of the separation between church and state reinforce the tendency to remove faith from the public arena. The church's role is understood as primarily to support individuals on their own personal spiritual journeys. One often hears comments that the church should avoid talk of politics. Speaking out about our responsibility to care for the earth always carries with it political and even partisan implications. Thus, ministers and church leaders who speak out on ecological issues will often find an immediate push back from some of their members.

Finally, contemporary apocalyptic images have also contributed to the tendency to ignore the earth's condition. Evangelical interpretations of Scripture that anticipate an imminent return of Jesus often lead to a sense of escapism, thus excusing us from the need to care for the earth. After all, if Christians are to be taken out of this world, then why should we be concerned about climate change, widespread pollution, or nuclear contamination? The popularity of books that promote these interpretations has prompted Christians (even those of us who are not inclined to expect a rapture to remove us from the earth's problems) to adopt a passive approach, at times bordering on helplessness, toward the environmental concerns that surround us.

To be fair, in recent years, some groups of evangelicals are becoming active in promoting creation care as central to Christian faith (e.g., consider the statement of faith of the Evangelical Environmental Network).[5] Many congregations, though, remain either unconcerned about issues like climate change or simply dismiss them as political causes that are unrelated to Christian faith.

To sum up, numerous influences have pushed the church away from a frontline leadership role in caring for creation. We are working from the theological positions that we inherited, including misinterpretations of Scripture and spiritual practices that detach us from the earth. In spite of calls to respond from leading theological voices, the church has been slow to engage in the work of environmental action.[6] Instead, many mainline churches are primarily preoccupied with their own survival. With declining memberships, many congregations have simply turned inward.

Perhaps, though, this is an opportunity for the church to look outward and work with others to address the ecological crises that confront us. Could the church's future be linked to the plight of the planet? With creation in crisis and the effects of climate change challenging our current patterns of consumption, the church must raise its voice by reappropriating, discovering, and embracing ways in which our worship practices cultivate a deep commitment to the earth. By immersing ourselves in caring for the world around us, we can rediscover our theological identity as part of God's good creation.

BACK TO THE BIBLE

In spite of the way Scripture has often been misinterpreted, it is the church's greatest resource to prompt us to care for the earth. In a recent class, I invited students to name biblical texts in which the earth played a central role. The list building began slowly with the creation stories and the psalms, but students gradually picked up the pace to include many of Jesus's parables, the stories of the exodus and wilderness wanderings of the ancient Israelites, the lavish images of the earth in the Song of Songs, the central place of the land in the Old Testament, and the promise of a new heaven and new earth with water flowing through it. From the opening pages of Genesis to the closing visions of the book of Revelation, the earth remains a central focus of the Bible.

The creation stories establish humanity's relationship to the earth. Even when one reads these accounts as a version of paradise lost, a story of sin and exile, they reflect nostalgia and longing to be in relationship with the earth. Adam and Eve carry with them the memory of living in harmony with the land. As their descendants, we maintain a distant memory of this relationship, of God walking in the garden with them.

Less literal readings of Genesis 1 and 2 picture creation as a delicate, interrelated ecosystem. God fashions human life out of the dust of the earth by breathing into it. Here, we see our deep connection to the basic elements of creation. In this portrait of paradise, humans are responsible for tending the garden and caring for the earth, plants, and animals. However, rather than assuming this role, man and woman long for more (the knowledge of good and evil) and place themselves at the center of the universe. Read from this perspective, the story of the exit from the Garden of Eden offers an opportunity for humans to discover their proper place in the world.

While these contrasting interpretations of Genesis come through different theological lenses, they both carry deep within them the importance of the earth as God's gift and of the human responsibility to care for it. Scripture connects us back to the narratives that enable us to see the world around us as God's good gift.

This sense of deep longing and connection to the earth as well as our desire to live in harmony with it is infused through Scripture and culminates in John's vision in the Book of Revelation of the new earth descending from heaven in order that paradise will be restored. Once again, the river of life runs through the city, and humans take their place with all of creation in singing praise to God.

Scripture uses the images of the earth to convey the story of God's abiding love of all creation. Thus, the first task for the church is to learn to listen again to the prominent place of creation in Scripture as it calls and prods us to see God's presence in the world around us. Once we become attuned to the many ways in which the authors of Scripture draw on earth images, then we will long for prayers and sermons that describe and explore ways that our lives can reflect this deep sense of connection between all of creation. Christian worship explores the innate connections between humans and the world around us.

BUILDING A FOUNDATION

With Scripture as the primary resource, how can we reclaim the earth as a central part of our worship? How can we use worship to help us discern our relationship and responsibility to the earth? Three options warrant review. First, many congregations focus on the importance of caring for the earth by celebrating an Earth Day service or another special occasion. Denominational offices and service organizations provide worship resources for use in these services.[7] This approach provides a good starting place for congregations to reconnect to the earth and discover ways to care for creation. At times, the worship resources appear to drive particular political agendas. A primary risk with this approach is that it can reinforce the sense that earth care, while important, only merits occasional emphasis rather than a role as a central component of Christian faith.

Recently, several liturgical scholars have advocated for a second option by adding an emphasis on creation to the liturgical year. One proposal calls for extending the season of Advent in a way that includes attention to justice and creation.[8] In the book *The Season of Creation,* a group of scholars in Australia and the United States offers the most fulsome plan to focus on different aspects of creation during the four Sundays of September. The proposal comes complete with an alternate set of lectionary readings for these Sundays. Each Sunday features a particular aspect of creation—for example, mountains or rivers.[9]

The strength of this approach is that it directs worshipers' attention for a month each year to particular aspects of creation during the worship service. Using biblical readings about creation is one way of highlighting the earth's importance in the Bible. The proposal includes readings from Scripture and commentaries on the texts to help preachers develop sermons that give particular attention to the theme of the day, but it does not provide specific liturgical suggestions. Still, while the authors of this proposal take great care to articulate the need for yearlong attention to creation care, they see this approach as an important step in the process of reorienting the church to see earth care as part of its primary mission.[10]

An additional strength of this proposal is that it makes space within the context of the larger framework of the Revised Common Lectionary and liturgical year to incorporate a time of sustained concentration on the earth. By creating a specific period of time within Ordinary Time, congregations maintain connection to the larger ecumenically shared calendars while still making room for a particular focus on the earth. This allows congregations to maintain ecumenical commitments and partnership that have grown by sharing liturgical calendars and lectionary texts while at the same time adding an emphasis on creation. Focusing on creation during September has an added advantage of connecting with a time in the life of many congregations when families return from summer vacation and Sunday school gears up for another year. Adding a particular emphasis on creation care at this time of year offers the possibility of concentrating congregational energy on the need to address environmental issues. Linking the themes to other activities in the life of the church provides an additional way of extending conversations and activities throughout the life of the congregation.

A potential drawback of this approach is the highly thematized nature of the proposal. While focusing on particular aspects of creation creates a greater awareness of the diversity of creation, it may ignore significant aspects of congregational life. For example, what are the pastoral care implications for congregations and individuals facing pressing needs when they show up to church to discover it is wilderness Sunday? Rather than listening for the earth's presence in Scripture and developing associations naturally, this highly choreographed approach thrusts distinct aspects of creation into the center of congregational life. In urban areas and particular parts of the country, people may find this particularly jarring. How does one properly celebrate Ocean Sunday in the middle of Kansas? While there is a need for a more holistic approach to the interrelated nature of all the earth, this approach strikes me as problematic, particularly in certain parts of the world.

Finally, I would add that the proposal detailed in *The Season of Creation* is not consistent with the overall purpose of the lectionary. The liturgical calendar is primarily Christocentric in its orientation. The annual journey from Advent to the Reign of Christ is primarily a way of marking time with the life, death, and resurrection of Jesus.

The proposal for a "season of creation," however, can be Christologically articulated. The authors write, for example, "Furthermore, insofar as Jesus belongs fully to Earth, God becomes incarnate in Earth." Extending the imagery of John 1 is one way to provide a bridge between a Christological orientation and the earth themes identified as focuses for the Sundays in the season of creation. While the authors may hold these theological connections, however, the practice of celebrating the earth and its resources moves in a different direction, and members in congregations may have difficulty seeing the ties. While attempting to extend the notion of incarnation to include the earth merits consideration, there remains a risk of obfuscating the church's central message of the liberating work of Jesus Christ.[11]

In contrast to these two approaches—designating either an occasional Sunday or a season when worship will focus on creation—I propose giving sustained attention throughout the year to caring for the earth. While these different approaches may be complementary, my particular concern is for Christians to learn a new hermeneutic, a new way of reading Scripture while looking at the world around them, and to see the earth and its health as integral to our Christian life and commitment. Hence, I am offering both a series of theological reflections on worship practices that incorporate elements of creation care as well as liturgical resources for the seasons of the church year, with a focus on images of the earth that complement each liturgical season.

Only when we reclaim the language and imagery of Scripture with its sustained attention to the earth as God's good gift will we be able to see that our Christian commitment that grows out of our baptismal vows includes caring for the earth. We need to give careful attention to both our language and action in worship so that our work for justice in creation grows out of our prayers and actions each day.

ADDITIONAL RESOURCES

We come to this task of reclaiming our relationship to the earth not only with Bibles in our hands, but with other assets for the journey. Since we often take these resources for granted, it is helpful to name them. One major resource is the many hymns and songs we sing that contain positive images of the earth. Historically, the importance placed on singing psalms in worship kept the language of the earth in the psalter prominent. From the early days when Christian gatherings in house churches followed Jewish practices of singing the psalms, to monastic communities that chanted the psalms during the prayers of the hours of the day, the use of the psalter maintained a connection to creation even at times when the interpretation of Scripture appeared highly spiritualized and disconnected from the earth. Reformation leaders such as John Calvin argued for the centrality of the psalms not only in worship services, but as part of the daily devotional practices of Christians in their homes. This practice reconnected Christians to the ancient practice of seeing the earth as the theater of God's glory.

Hymnody and song often use direct quotes, paraphrases, or imagery from Scripture, including language of creation. Traditional hymns like "All Creatures of Our God and King" and "For the Beauty of the Earth" speak of the grandeur of the earth and ways in which our own praise echoes that of creation. Similarly, praise songs such as "God of Wonders" or "Shout to the Lord, All the Earth" invite worshipers to see the world around us as calling out in thanksgiving to God.

Here, though, a word of caution is necessary. Worship leaders should ensure that our references to the earth are not exclusively romantic, like much of the language hymnody and song employs.[12] While joining our voices with all of creation in praising God has a central place in our gatherings, there is a risk of reinforcing a naïve view of nature that all is always idyllic in the world. In this time of dramatic climate change and environmental disasters, Christians must honestly represent both the beauty and the pain of creation. Including regular opportunities for both thanksgiving and supplication for the earth during the prayers of the people provides an important way to create greater awareness and connections. Skillful use of technology can provide a fuller portrait by presenting pictures of the beauty of the earth while also showing us places where the "whole creation groans and travails in pain" (Romans 8:22).

Using photographs from local areas in worship services is a particularly effective way of teaching Christians that faith relates to our appreciation of and care for this part of the earth on which we live. While building global awareness is important, solely using stock photos found on the Web, which may have appeal in terms of both aesthetic quality and dramatic impact, runs the risk of encouraging us to overlook this part of the earth that we live in, walk on, and rely on each and every day. Cultivating a sense of the beauty and the needs of the land and water close to us, which we often take for granted, is one important way of bringing the world into our sanctuaries. Local pictures taken by members of the congregation also provide a personal perspective on the world around us. Here, our relationship to the earth as seen in photographs provides a form of testimony about how Christians relate to and respond to the needs of the earth.

Using objects from nature is another significant way of bringing the world into our sanctuaries. Invite people in your congregation to bring something natural that they found on a recent walk—a rock, shells, acorns, leaves in the fall. Times of prayer can include inviting people to bring their objects to the front of the sanctuary as a way of expressing thanks for the beauty and diversity of creation. I recently preached a sermon on the importance of water both in the church and in the world, and I brought a pitcher of water that I collected from the James River and poured it in the font. Here, the cleanliness of water in the baptismal font was immediately connected to the condition of the water in the local river. The options are endless and offer thoughtful worship planners opportunities to connect the earth and the changing seasons to the space in which we gather for worship.

Worship is not simply one aspect of congregational life. Worship is the center of the church's actions. Congregational renewal that is centered in worship seeks to show how the church's other gatherings grow out of our worship of God. How does Sunday morning help us look at our congregation's priorities, commitments, and belongings in light of the Gospel and the needs of our community? One of the most underutilized resources in most congregations is the church property itself. How can worship draw on the resources of the church property to highlight the need to care for the earth?

Take some time to ask yourself questions about how your congregation's practices of creation care are evident as you look at the church and the surrounding property. How do we care for this part of the earth on which we have built a church? What do we plant on our grounds and how do we care for it? How much of the property do we pave over for parking, and what concerns do we have about water run-off? How we treat the property that churches own is a primary testimony to ways that faith relates or ignores creation care.

Years ago, biblical scholar Ched Myers spoke about using congregational resources to respond to the needs of our communities. Allowing a farmer's market to use the church parking lot or serving as a pick-up point for a community supported agriculture (CSA) project connects local farmers with people in the neighborhood. The financial cost to the church is minimal while the exposure is significant, providing a way for people in the neighborhood to learn more about what is going on in the life of your congregation. More importantly, these activities provide opportunities to welcome and get to know people in your neighborhood.

First Presbyterian Church in Newport, Oregon, on the Pacific coast, created a community garden on its property several years ago. They invited people in the surrounding area to plant and tend the garden to grow food for their own use. In recent years, the practice has extended to include church members who grow food in the church's garden and then donate the produce to the community food bank that is housed on the church property. Here is one way that congregations can claim their own land as a gift not simply for their own private use, but as an opportunity to practice hospitality and model earth care as integral to Christian faith.

One final resource to consider is the church's finances. Budgets are moral documents that reveal our priorities. How does our use of money reflect the importance that we place on caring for the earth? Even in times when church budgets are tight, we can ask, what is it that we value most highly? Are we practicing what we preach? Do we designate financial resources to minimize our carbon imprint when we come to worship and other gatherings? Are we willing to invest in alternative sources of energy? Examining church finances and making adjustments is an important endeavor for Christian communities to show a renewed commitment to the earth.

The church has a vast number of assets for this important task of strengthening our relationship to the earth as we gather for worship and other opportunities for learning and engagement in the community that grow out of its worship life. From our reading of Scripture to the hymns and songs we sing, from the ways we enjoy and care for the earth to our use of objects in the world around us, from the ways that we care for church properties to our willingness to share our building and land with other groups, congregations have access to rich resources that will enable them to play a leading role in advocating for justice and living in harmony with the world around us.

An even more important resource for us to consider, however, is ourselves. In the next chapter, we turn our attention to the important work of naming and recognizing our practices of earth care as a central part of life in our communities of faith.

Chapter 1

Liturgical Resources

ADVENT

Call to Worship

Shine a light in the darkness.
Make the path straight.
Bind up the weary and brokenhearted.
Welcome strangers and all those whom feel neglected.
Let us prepare for the coming of the Christ child.

Prayer of the Day

Faithful God, creator of our days, from morning light to the stars in the night,
Your creation reveals your promises, still enduring through the ages.
Renew us in hope as the morning renews us,
   that we may live alert to the dawning of new life,
Waiting with expectation to be reunited with Jesus Christ, our Savior and judge,
   who lives and reigns with You in the unity of the Holy Spirit,
   Three in One, One in Three, now and forever.
Amen.

Confession and Pardon

Come, all who long for wholeness.
Come, all who yearn to grow.
Come, all who seek to flourish.
Here, Christ awaits us to heal us, restore us, and renew us.
Let us confess our sin to God and to one another.

Gracious God, we confess that we often turn from you and from our neighbor and live in despair of creating a world of hope and possibility. Forgive us for relying on our own ambition rather than allowing faith to take root and grow in our lives. Water us with your Word, that our souls may be refreshed and we may come to life. Gather us in and care for us, that we may share your blessing with all who long for your presence, through Christ we pray, Amen.

Hear these words from Scripture: The reign of God is like a woman baking bread who mixes a little yeast into the dough. As the yeast ferments and the bread rises, so too God's grace grows in our lives, so that we may flourish, and work for a world of peace and harmony. In the water of baptism, we are claimed as part of God's good creation. Let us live and work together for a community of hope and justice.

Prayer for Illumination

Come, Holy Spirit, and bring light in our darkness.
Help us as we hear your Word, to welcome and nourish it
so that your vision of new life will take root in our lives, through Christ we pray.
Amen.

Prayer of Dedication

God of all life, receive the gifts that we offer here today,
the gifts of time, of money, and of ourselves.
Grant us your blessing that we may grow in faith and provide a place of respite and hope.
Make us signs of your new creation, through Christ, the One who brings us life and light.
Amen.

ADVENT EUCHARIST

Scripture: Meal images from Luke 13–14

Invitation to the Lord's Table

The day is coming when
"People will come from east and west,
From north and south,
And will eat in the kingdom of God.
Indeed, some are last who will be first,
And some are first who will be last."
Come to this table to learn of the days to come.
All who yearn for a new day and new life are welcome in this place.

Great Thanksgiving

The Lord be with you.
And also with you.
Lift up your hearts.
We lift them up to the Lord.
Let us give thanks to God.
It is good to give our thanks and praise.

Creating God, the earth and sky show us signs of your glory in the trees that
reach up to the sky and in the stars that shine down upon us.
You fashioned us from the soil to live in your image and to care for creation.
When we turned away from you to follow our own selfish interests,
You called us back with the songs of creations, the voices of prophets, and the
testimonies of our ancestors.
In Jesus Christ, your Word came among us to point us again in the way of life.
And so we join our voices to sing your praise with all of creation:

Holy, holy, holy Lord,
God of power and might.
Heaven and earth are full of your glory.
Hosanna in the highest.
Blessed is the one who comes in the name of the Lord.
Hosanna in the highest.

Your holiness surrounds us and beckons us to live as Jesus showed us:
To invite the poor, the crippled, the lame, and the blind
to come to the table and to share this meal with us.
In his life, he offered hope.
In his death, he offered himself.
In his resurrection, you raised him to new life.

* * *

With grateful hearts, we receive these gifts of bread and wine from the earth
And share them as a way of welcoming all to live in harmony with you, with
one another, and with the earth.
Receive us and this prayer as an expression of our dependence on you for each
breath of life that you give us.

Great is the mystery of faith:
Christ has died.
Christ is risen.
Christ will come again.

Make your Spirit present to us in our lives
through the sharing of this bread and this cup.
Plant within us faith like a mustard seed
That we may grow into a community that is rooted in this earth
And that honors all of creation.
Help us to gather in those who are neglected and forgotten
That we may be a sign of your coming reign.
Renew our hope that we may yearn and work for the season of your coming
When peace and justice will reign.
Through Christ, with Christ, in Christ, by the presence of your Spirit. Amen.

The Lord's Prayer
Breaking of the Bread

As Jesus broke bread and shared a cup with all manner of people,
So too we share this meal with all who yearn for a new day where justice will
roll down like waters and righteousness like an ever-flowing stream.
These are God's gifts to sustain us on our journey.

Chapter Two

Seeing Our Place in the World

At a Native American church I visited on a recent sabbatical, Richard took me aside to tell me his story. Life had been hard for him, and he was struggling to get back on his feet after spending time in a local treatment center. He had come back to church and was trying to keep his life moving in a positive direction. He prayed daily for work, so he could take care of his family and pay his bills, but good jobs were hard to come by on the reservation. One morning, he went out canoeing on the river. He paddled his way down a stream alongside riverbanks lined by cedar trees, an ancient sign of divine presence for Native Americans. Far from civilization, his cell phone unexpectedly rang, and he was invited to interview for a school job (that he would later get). In his account, the cedar trees surrounding him, looked down upon him, and bowed in the breeze as a sign of God's favor. The blessings of nature provided a context in which his hopes and dreams came to fruition. Even the unlikely event of having a cell phone signal in the wilderness provided a deep sense of God's provision in his life.

While such a story may be more poignant than most, I discovered during my sabbatical that it was not altogether unusual. I spent a year in the Pacific Northwest listening to members of six diverse Presbyterian congregations talk to me about their experiences in nature and their commitment to caring for the earth. The congregations ranged theologically from highly evangelical to fairly progressive. They were located in urban, suburban, and small town settings, and measured by worship attendance, they ranged from small to midsized. Two of the six congregations were what Presbyterians call "racial-ethnic," in this case, a Native American and a Cambodian congregation. In spite of the wide range of differences, I consistently encountered people who longed to talk with me about their deep sense of connection to the earth and their personal commitment to caring for it. Sharing these stories provided an avenue for them to name places where they had encountered the presence of God in nature and to explore ways of connecting these experiences to their communities of faith. In groups and with individuals, I asked simple questions about creation-care practices and how they relate to faith and worship. I was struck by the willingness of people to speak openly and passionately about significant experiences of the divine in nature and about their commitment to caring for the earth. Even so, most people had not consciously associated their ecological activities with their faith.

As congregations begin the difficult work of reconnecting Christian faith to the gift and rhythms of the earth, members' experiences of nature provide a great starting point for exploring ways of relating these experiences to the church's work and witness—for the important work of making room for and encouraging people to tell their stories in our congregations. I had the opportunity to listen to people in congregations learn to view seeing their earth care practices in light of their faith.

People in the Pacific Northwest tend to have a special connection to the dramatic beauty of nature that surrounds them. Across Oregon, Washington, and British Columbia, the stunning mountains, the picturesque forests, and the pounding waves of the Pacific Ocean on the breathtaking coast beckon to both people of faith and people of no faith. In *Cascadia: The Elusive Utopia,* fourteen authors from a broad range of disciplines describe their spirituality in terms of a connection to nature that people in this region share. One contributor qualifies this understanding: "But, in Cascadia, in the Pacific Nation, we prefer spirituality to religion. We like to be breathed into, to be, as they say, inspired."[1]

Although they came from different backgrounds and perspectives, church members were inspired by the beauty of the surrounding world. They shared a common ethos and outlook in their perspectives on the beauty of nature as a testimony to the grandeur of God's creation, and they saw signs of God's presence in the world around them. Although many sermons and prayers do not include references to nature, I was surprised at the eagerness people exhibited to talk about their experiences in nature and to link it to their faith.

While the Pacific Northwest is a unique place where people have deep ties to the land, one can find similar attachments to the earth in conversations with people in other regions—people who appreciate the stark beauty of the vast Midwestern plains or those who love the high desert country of New Mexico. While I provide examples here of the stories that I heard from people in the Pacific Northwest, you will find similar stories of appreciation for the beauty of the earth in your own congregation.

CULTIVATING APPRECIATION

People regularly spoke about their sense of awe in nature. Whether they felt the pounding surf on the beach or viewed the snow-capped mountains, they were deeply and regularly moved by the beauty of the world around them. Along with a concern that ongoing development and industrialization threatened nature, they expressed an awareness that they should not take the earth for granted. Many individuals interpreted the simple act of taking walks in the woods as a form of devotion or embodied prayer.

Another regular observation offered by people I interviewed centered on a new perspective of oneself acquired in nature. Standing in the middle of a vast national forest, one feels small. Instead of seeing oneself or humans as the center of the universe or even the top of the chain of life, we discover a sense of kinship in nature and see ourselves as part of the universe around us. People spoke of the importance of respecting nature and of valuing the earth in all its diversity. They observed that by actively involving ourselves in caring for the earth, we move beyond a simple understanding of the beauty of creation (nature as a postcard) to a greater awareness of the power, danger, and wildness of life that surrounds us.

Many people also spoke about how their growing awareness of our place in a vast universe increased their appreciation of the earth and the interrelatedness of all of creation. Native Americans spoke about how humans learned to live by watching the animals. Stories handed down by their ancestors describe how humans learned to drum and sing by listening to the animals. Humans discovered how to travel by following the movements of animals in order to find food and shelter. In other congregations, individuals described ways that their experiences in nature led to a greater understanding of how our choices and actions impact all the world. In nature, they learned to see the earth as an ecosystem with deep connections among the vastly diverse forms of life. These experiences created a deeper sensitivity to the importance of lessening their impact on the planet.

ACTS OF CARING

Members from all of the congregations in this study spoke about the importance of changing personal habits and practices in order to care for creation. In predominantly white congregations, the lists of environmental actions often began with the familiar: recycling and composting, changing to energy-efficient light bulbs and alternative sources (solar and wind) for energy, using green products for cleaning and gardening (avoiding toxic chemicals and pesticides), conserving water, relying less on automobiles (and/or using hybrids), changing eating habits (consuming less meat and more fruits and vegetables), and purchasing local, organic food products. From these initial steps, people branched out to explore additional ways that they could minimize their impact on the land.

In this list of actions, one can readily see the influence of the environmental movement pressing us to change our daily habits in order to limit our impact on the earth. Mainstream cultural influences (especially on the West Coast) prompt individuals to reexamine their patterns of living and to make adjustments for the well-being of the planet. In some instances, these changes involve minor patterns (buying organic rather than conventional produce), while at other times they require major commitments. (One individual had served as a volunteer warden, picking up trash at a city park for 22 years.)

Members of the Cambodian and Native American communities approached the topic from a different perspective. Instead of starting from a list of ecological actions created by environmental groups, they tended to begin from the point of the view of the earth. Cambodians spoke about honoring nature—the trees that give us oxygen and the fertile soil that gives us life. One member spoke of the importance of blessing seeds, so they would grow and produce food to eat. Similarly, Native Americans described the value of living lightly on the earth by using only what one needs. Others spoke of the ancient wisdom of their elders, who taught that the forces of nature, wind and water, come from the Great Spirit. Respect for Mother Earth requires us to exercise caution and limit the ways that we use the land. Extending from this base, some individuals described practices of recycling and simplified living as important ways to live in harmony with the earth.

Both Cambodian and Native American Christians drew primarily from their cultural backgrounds and histories when framing their reasons for caring for the earth. Cambodians articulated Buddhist perspectives on the sanctity of all life forms and the significance of respecting the earth. Native Americans referenced the teaching of their elders and the wisdom of native spirituality's notions that Mother Earth is sacred, that the Great Spirit animates all of creation. Surprisingly, while members of both these congregations are theologically conservative and in many instances take great care to distance themselves from their cultural and spiritual backgrounds, when it came to articulating reasons to care for the earth, they relied on the language of their earlier religious identities.[2]

In general, the people I talked with did not articulate specific Christian reasons for caring for the earth. I could have heard similar accounts at a local meeting of the Sierra Club. While individual Christians were concerned with changing their habits in order to lessen the impact on the earth, in the end their actions were primarily framed by other cultural influences—from the environmental movement to other religious traditions. I was left wondering how Christians can offer a unique theological rationale for our care for the earth. How can we learn to connect our practices of creation care with the reading of Scripture and the language of prayer?

I interviewed some individuals who found ways to tie their personal practices to Christian faith. Keith lives in a house in a gated community near the Oregon Coast. His early concerns about environmental matters centered on storm water drainage and damage caused by chemicals in water runoff. Financial problems caused the company developing the land surrounding his home to stop further work on the subdivision. Each morning, Keith would look out on the parcel of land next to his house. He felt pain as he looked out on the scarred, barren land that had been bulldozed in preparation for building, only to be abandoned. Finally, he could stand the situation no longer. He decided to buy the plot next to him and restore it to its natural habitat. For ten years, he has worked on the land, planting cedar, hemlock, and spruce seedlings. As the trees have grown, he has created paths through the woods and even placed a prayer bench in one opening, where he spends time meditating and reflecting each day. In describing his work, he uses religious language: creating a sanctuary, seeing the land as a place of meditation and a source of inspiration, expressing gratitude for God's presence in the beauty of this place. In his work of caring for the land, Keith has created connections between his love of and desire to care for the earth, and his Christian faith. No one in church has explicitly taught or modeled these ties. Instead, he has developed them on his own. A host of personal influences have come together to sustain and inspire him as he has toiled on the land.

Individuals in our congregations are beginning to make connections between their faith and their practices of creation care, and many people talk about feeling responsibility to care for God's creation. By and large, though, pastors and church leaders have left them on their own to make these associations. General religious language, including the words of our liturgies and prayers, provides vague guidance. Broad language that endorses caring for our neighbor provides a framework for developing interdependence. Worshipers may interpret Jesus's great commandment to love our neighbor as we love ourselves as a reason to limit consumption and to conserve the earth's resources for future generations. Often stewardship language reinforces this sense of responsibility and duty to avoid causing long-term damage to the environment. Certain individuals extrapolate further to connect these words to the actions of preserving habitat for other forms of life and allowing the beauty and diversity of the earth to flourish for the benefit of future generations.

In general, however, congregations say little about how our faith informs our understanding of creation. In a 2013 survey, historian Samuel Torvend analyzes prayers from worship books of different denominations, examining where and how language of creation shows up in worship resources. He concludes that while there has been a limited increase in the use of creation language in our liturgies since the reforms of Vatican II, the prayers "lack an ethical dimension," particularly following the communion prayer.[3] While there are limited references in our liturgies to creation care, little attention is given to showing worshipers what shape these prayers can take in our lives.

LOOKING FOR LEADERSHIP

Listening to members of congregations talk about ways that they care for the earth shows me that many are eager and willing to talk about their own commitment and practice. However, a simple question such as, "How does Christian faith prompt your care for the earth?" leaves them scrambling to describe their connections in anything more than general platitudes. Clearly, congregations need to offer more education and opportunities for people to share their concerns and ideas with one another. Pastors and Christian educators can serve an important role in prompting these conversations and in helping develop theological rationale for the actions that people carry out in their daily lives. Because of the historic separation between sacred and secular domains, we often train people to use language that embodies a personal (and sometimes private) spirituality that we adopt from religious leaders whom we perceive as experts in the field. When congregational members leave our church buildings, in many ways they are left on their own to correlate their daily actions with faith by using their own resources, apart from anything they have done or heard in church.

In his brilliant book *Earth-honoring Faith,* Christian ethicist Larry Rasmussen describes the work that the church needs to do to respond to the environmental crisis, arguing that this task requires a dramatic change in the way we see and interact with the world around us. Cultivating dimensions of Christian faith that encourage us to respond to the pressing needs of the earth will require us to acknowledge the integral connection between Christian faith and the earth. Rasmussen's approach builds on the insights of the great German theologian Dietrich Bonhoeffer, who rejected an "otherworldly Christianity," and insisted that Christian communities dedicate themselves to the task of building God's kingdom on this earth.[4] Here Christian responsibility to care for God's creation is grounded in the hope and belief that our redemption is tied up in the fate of all of creation.

The task of pastors and congregational leaders is to help instill in the life of the congregation an ethic of love and respect for the earth as a central value of Christian faith and life. This ethic shifts from a primary occupation with the human condition to a concern about all of life in the universe. Rasmussen describes this shift as a move from "the ego to the ecosphere."[5] We learn that our own fate is integrally linked to the well-being of all creation. Ethicist James Smith observes that "we have a 'feel' for the world that is informed by stories [and practices] that dispose us to inhabit the world as *either* a bounteous but broken gift of the Creator *or* as a closed system of scarcity and competition."[6]

An earth-honoring ethic provides a theological foundation beneath our earth-care practices. In this work, the sacraments of baptism and communion provide occasions for communities of faith to gather and rehearse this move from ego- to eco-centered lives. As Christians, we take this water from the earth and this bread from the wheat of the ground and these grapes nourished by the sun and the earth's soil to declare God's faithfulness and to cultivate gratitude and thanksgiving in our lives. We celebrate these sacraments with our bodies as we gather in this place, around this table, next to one another, and share the earth's gifts of water, bread, and wine. In these acts, we learn to rely on God's grace and the Spirit's presence in one another, in this stuff that comes from the earth, and in our own lives. Here, at table and font, we encounter Christ's presence and receive grace for our journey. Here, we practice a dramatic move from self-reliance to trust in the divine presence that is woven throughout creation. This transformative work requires church leaders, clergy and lay, to encourage members of the congregation to gather regularly, share stories of our experiences in nature, encourage practices of creation care, prompt questions about our choices and habits, and point to biblical and theological resources that will undergird and sustain us in this dramatic shift.

Learning to see the world around us differently requires us to use our imaginations as we move from the perspective that the earth exists to provide what we need, to an experience of the earth as our partner and home. Approaching this change through our celebration of the sacraments provides the church with a unique voice as we partner with all who work to preserve, honor, and protect the earth and her abundant resources. Recognizing that the celebration of the sacraments draws from the earth's resource demands that our theology of redemption encompasses the redemption of all creation.

Pastors and educators can assist church members in gaining a new perspective on ourselves and our relationship to the earth by cultivating a sacramental imagination. Conversations can start with simple questions: How do we see the world around us in light of our experiences at the table and font? How do these experiences prompt us to tell our own stories of encountering God in nature? How do we listen to Scripture in light of these experiences? Often, we are trained to read the Bible primarily as a historical document that is intended to inform our beliefs. Cultivating a sacramental imagination allows us to hear Scripture as a primary witness to the ways we encounter God's presence that are implicit in the ways we gather around table and font and as we experience the Spirit in the beauty of creation. In this setting, we learn to observe the world around us and imagine our place in it from the perspective of sacred stories and practices that we share together.[7]

Preachers and educators can help point out the ways that our participation in the world and care for creation grow out of a shared faith commitment. We invite one another to share stories and describe our practices of caring for creation in order to discern how our actions and choices each day embody our Christian faith and values. Effective leaders work at multiple levels in these conversations by pointing to connections between biblical narratives and our own practices of caring for creation, and by lifting up and framing theological virtues that are implicit in our stories. This hard work uncovers ways in which Christian faith takes shape in our daily lives.

SACRAMENTAL APPROACHES TO PREACHING

Preaching in particular provides ample opportunities for showing how Scripture presents sacramental images of the earth and our place in it. Preachers who experience the sacraments as encounters with the divine can practice this sacramental imagination in their interpretation of texts.[8] Nurturing the sacramental imagination of congregational members through preaching requires us to move beyond the reading of Scripture from the primary perspective of the historical-critical method. To accomplish this goal, preachers must develop the skill of recognizing associations between the text and the place of the sacraments and the earth in the life of our communities of faith. The Revised Common Lectionary models this approach by assuming a correlation between meal stories in Scripture and the celebration of communion.

For several semesters, I gave students in my classes on the sacraments an assignment of writing a journal on sacramental images they found in their readings of Scripture from the daily lectionary. The results of this exercise followed a pattern. During the first month, the majority of students were unwilling to make associations between Scripture readings and the sacraments. Their training in exegesis and interpretation in their Bible classes made them reluctant to discern sacramental dimensions of the text. For example, when reflecting on the Exodus narrative of the Hebrew children crossing the Red Sea, students noted that while the text included references to water and deliverance to new life, it would be inappropriate to read Christian themes of baptism into this passage from the Hebrew Scripture. By the third month of this exercise, students began to develop the skill of seeing different layers in texts and identifying ways in which the sacraments and the earth permeate Scripture. This process of cultivating a sacramental imagination lies at the center of this approach to preaching. The preacher's own commitment to the sacramental life of the church models and encourages imaginative ways of reading Scripture in which the sacraments serve as primary focal points for the community's life together. In this sense, we can call "liturgical preaching" the deliberative art of speaking about Scripture in ways that provide patterns for the congregation's own reading of Scripture. The preacher demonstrates how biblical texts connect to the earth and our own lives.

In a recent survey done by the research office in the Presbyterian Church (U.S.A.), pastors and members were asked to indicate the degree of relevance between selected Bible passages and the Lord's Supper. Predictably, seen as most relevant were two texts often associated with Jesus's Last Supper: Luke 22:19 ("Do this in remembrance of me") and 1 Corinthians 11:26 ("As often as you eat this bread"). Since participants had been given a list of texts deemed potentially relevant, there are already restrictions on what texts are deemed relevant to the Sacraments. Little room is left for any imaginative associations between the Sacraments and Scripture.

What is shocking from the results of the survey is that texts with clear Eucharistic imagery were largely ignored and overlooked. Less than one third of the members of the congregations (32 percent) and just over one half of the pastors (54 percent) saw the Acts 2 narrative of the early church's practice of breaking bread with glad and generous hearts as very significant or significant to the celebration of communion. Similarly, Luke 24 (the road to Emmaus) was rated as very significant or significant by only 31 percent of members and 66 percent of pastors. Jesus's resurrection meal with the disciples in John 21 was not even included on the original list of texts!

Similarly shocking results are found in the results from questions about Scripture and baptism. Nearly three-fourths of the members and pastors identified Jesus welcoming the little children in Matthew 19 as very significant or significant, presumably because this text is often used to support the practice of infant baptism (even though a reading of this text shows little interest in baptismal themes). Yet, texts with imaginative or other associative connections to water and baptism, such as the story about the woman at the well in John 4, were not even part of the survey.[9]

If we are going to learn the art of seeing the world sacramentally, then we must learn a new way of reading and hearing Scripture. Preaching can help us move away from primarily cognitive and rational explanations, and invite listeners to discover the possibility of encountering the divine in and through these ordinary things around which we gather: this book, this water, this bread and wine. Rather than articulating the "proper meaning" of a text in light of its historical background, liturgical preaching makes room for and invites listeners to develop and exercise imaginative associations with a particular text.

In this regard, I am not proposing that we abandon theological arguments and careful exegesis of Scripture. Instead, I am urging that these acts be accompanied by reflection on the ways that biblical texts connect to the sacramental practices that sustain the lives of our communities and help us to name God's presence in the world around us.

Liturgical preachers are not content to reside within the safe confines of church walls. Instead, they recognize the congregation's gathering space as a place to start in reclaiming the assembly's full participation in the incarnational work of the Gospel in the world. As Western culture continues the process of throwing off the cloak of Christendom, many congregations are increasingly aware that the church now exists on the margins of society rather than at the center of culture.

In order to survive, congregations must give up their nostalgia for the way things used to be, as well as the temptation to isolate ourselves from the world around us. Liturgical preaching can point us in a new direction. Rather than allowing us to retreat from the world to the splendid isolation of our sanctuaries, liturgical preaching places us in the world in order that we may encounter the risen Christ beyond the walls of our church buildings. By teaching us to read and hear texts in new ways, by cultivating a sacramental imagination, by stressing the primary role of community in an age of individualism and privatism, liturgical preaching uncovers and creates associations between the liturgy, the assembly, and the world around us. These actions help congregations discover connections between faith and creation care.

Gathering for worship is not simply an act of preparing to go forth from the church into the world. The church is not somehow a place separate from the world, a place where we retreat from the world and to which we return. Liturgical preaching that emphasizes the connection of biblical texts with the ordinary things of the sacraments and the ordinary things of our lives provides an important corrective to Christian speech that often simply relies on otherworldly, spiritual language. Here the church is envisioned not as a place apart from the world around us, a place where we go for correction and instruction about how to survive out there in the world. Rather, the church as the body of Christ serves as an incarnational sign *in* the world.

Liturgical preaching underscores the physicality of our bodies, this place, and these things around which we gather in the hope and possibility that, like the disciples on the road to Emmaus, our eyes might be opened in the breaking of the bread. Liturgy as an embodied act demonstrates how we relate to one another and to the world around us. Our response to the Gospel is a physical, incarnational act of our bodies.

Liturgical theologian Cláudio Carvalhaes describes the resistance to speaking of our bodies as central to Christian faith in his essay, "'Gimme de kneebone bent': Liturgics, Dance, Resistance and a Hermeneutics of the Knees," "The knees have always been a dangerous element in the Christian faith. In spite of the doctrine of the incarnation, God's *excessive knee movement* in Christ, the Christian body in general remained a frightened space where things can easily get out of control."[10]

Liturgical preaching works to reclaim our bodies as a primary locus of God's ongoing act of creation, in which our connections to one another, the earth, and all of God's good creation are signs of faithful discipleship. The embodied preacher raises her voice and points to times and places where our bodies prompt our imaginations to see the Spirit at work in our lives. This radical act of reclaiming space for our bodies in worship leads Carvalhaes to conclude that the church must involve our bodies in worship. Starting with the knees

> is just the first stop on this road hermeneutics of the body, an approach that should be always corrected by other knee movements and thoughts. Then we should take on [Latin American pop artist] Shakira's suggestions and deconstruct the hips, then the hands, the feet, the hair, the belly, the eyes, the mouth, the vagina, the neck, the penis, the skin and so on. [11]

The goal here is for every part of our body (especially those parts that we are reluctant to name in "good Christian gatherings") to worship God. Liturgical preaching invites us body, mind, and soul to respond to Christ's invitation to "follow me." This disruptive process invites us out of the passive posture of sitting in our pews and into a full-bodied response to the Word who was made flesh and dwelt among us. In these incarnational movements, liturgical preaching brings together text, sacrament, assembly, earth, and space in order that we may see and encounter the One who shows us the way, truth, and life.

In the end, through the work of the Holy Spirit, the goal of all preaching is transformation—namely, that through an encounter with this text, in this place, with these people, we may discover a new way to look at ourselves and the world around us. This requires a process of conversion in which we experience the disruptive power of grace that changes our vision. Liturgical preaching provides a particular set of lenses that foster the development of this new sight.

Years ago, I read a psychological study of an experiment in which subjects were given a set of glasses that caused them to see the world upside down. As a part of the study, the subjects were required to wear the glasses every day for one week. In the initial days, the subjects reported the expected difficulties of disorientation, such as walking into objects. However, in a relatively short period of time, the subjects had learned to navigate according to this new way of seeing the world. At the end of the study, when they took off the glasses, they experienced disorientation similar to their first days wearing them and needed time to readapt to another way of seeing the world around them.

Learning to see the world in a new way takes time. The philosopher Ludwig Wittgenstein once observed, "I wanted to put this picture before your eyes, and your *acceptance* of this picture consists in your being inclined to regard a given case differently; that is, to compare it with *this* series of pictures. I have changed your *way of seeing*." [12]

Liturgical preaching presents the claims of Scripture on our lives in the context of the worshipping assembly in order that we may experience a new way of seeing and respond to the call to discipleship.

Telling our stories of encountering God in creation and learning to hear the stories of Scripture in a new way are central ingredients in the transition that is required in order for Christians to reclaim our voices in the work of creation care. Placing these narratives side by side as we gather around the font and table is a way to integrate the experiences of our daily lives with the promise of Christ's presence. Leaders who learn to consider these diverse experiences and testimonies alongside biblical texts support congregations in reconnecting Christian faith to the rhythms of the earth.

Liturgical Resources

CHRISTMAS

Glory to God in the highest.
Peace and good will on earth.
O come, let us adore him.
Christ, the Lord of all creation.

Prayer of the Day

Almighty God, you who wonderfully created all of nature,
Who in the incarnation of your Son presented your presence and your hope,
In your mercy let us live as redeemed members of your creation,
    in harmony with your good created world.
Teach us the humility of your incarnate Son
    who as an infant slept among the animals of your creation,
        that we might live rightly with all living things.
Through your incarnate Son, our Lord, by the power of the Holy Spirit.
Amen.

Confession and Pardon

Let us turn from our brokenness and isolation from one another and from creation.
Let us come and see what the Lord has made known to us.
In faith, let us confess our sin to God and to one another.

Immanuel, God with us,
We have seen your stars in the sky and yet turned away from your light.
We have heard the songs of creation praising you and yet ignored your call to follow.
In your mercy, forgive us so that our voices will join with all creation in glorifying and praising you. Amen.

Hear these words of Scripture: "Do not be afraid; for see—I am bringing you good news of great joy for all people; to you is born this day in the city of David, a Savior who is Christ the Lord." Christ Jesus who comes to dwell among us will bring us peace. **Amen.**

Prayer for Illumination

Incarnate God, may your word be born in us today,
may we treasure and ponder it in our hearts,
and may we grow in wisdom and stature and in divine and human favor.
Amen.

Prayer of Dedication

We give you thanks, God, for all of your gifts: for creation and the beauty of
this earth,
For the Christ child who shows us your way,
For the church that points to your presence in our lives.
May our gifts of time, money, and ourselves help us to share your good news
with all the earth. Amen.

CHRISTMAS EUCHARIST

Scripture: Meal images from Luke 2 and Feeding of 5,000 (Luke 9)

Come, all who are hungry.
Come, all who long to be filled.
Come and share this meal together.
At this table, Christ is present among us and brings us new life.

The Lord be with you.
And also with you.
Lift up your hearts.
We lift them up to the Lord.
Let us give thanks to God.
It is good to give our thanks and praise.

Creating God,
You made the heavens and stars to show forth your glory.
In your image, you fashioned us by breathing life into us and invited us to care for one another and your creation.
When we turned away from you, your presence continued to shine among us.
You sent prophets to point us to your way and psalmists to teach us songs of praise.
In the fullness of time, your Son was born among us, full of grace and truth.
So we join our voices with all who sing of your glory:

Holy, holy, holy Lord,
God of power and might.
Heaven and earth are full of your glory.
Hosanna in the highest.
Blessed is the one who comes in the name of the Lord.
Hosanna in the highest.

We give you thanks for the gift of the Christ child:
Born in a manger, nursed at Mary's breast,
taught by Joseph, drenched in the Spirit.
In a deserted place, he broke bread and shared it with all who were hungry.
He healed the sick and welcomed strangers.
When he was crucified on a cross, you raised him to new life.

* * *

Remembering the generous ways that you nourish us
We take this bread and cup
And share them with all who hunger and thirst.
Receive us and fill us with your gifts that our lives may be signs of your grace.

Great is the mystery of faith:
Christ has died.
Christ is risen.
Christ will come again.

Send your Spirit on us and this bread and cup
That we may receive your blessing
And share it with all who are around us.
Lead us into the world to work to feed the hungry,
to bring healing to creation,
and to reconcile enemies.
Fill us with your songs of praise
that we may sing of your glory and work for your peace.
Through Christ, with Christ, in Christ. Amen.

The Lord's Prayer
Breaking of the Bread

Jesus took the loaves and looked up to heaven,
And blessed them and broke them,
And gave them to the disciples to share with all.
These are the gifts of God for the people of God.

Chapter Three

Meals, Values, and the Earth

What practices will support us as we share our lives and change the vision of our place in the cosmos? In previous chapters, we examined the important task of reclaiming the central place of the earth as it is honored throughout Scripture, from the opening chapters of Genesis to the closing vision of Revelation. In recent years, numerous scholars have underscored the need to develop theological resources that reappropriate the foundational role of Scripture in caring for the earth. Sources like the Earth Bible present the work of scholars who have reexamined accepted readings of Scripture and argued for the importance of giving special attention to the place of the earth in biblical texts in light of a hermeneutic of eco-justice. Taking us beyond the clever color coding of the Earth Bible (it designates earth passages with light green print), a rereading of Scripture from the perspective of the earth and its needs provides an important starting place for congregations to engage in the hard work of aligning the witness of Scripture with their ministry to the needs of the world.[1]

In this chapter, I am proposing that the meal stories of the Gospels and the Acts of the Apostles can serve as a guide in our work of caring for the earth. The goal is to show how the practices of creation care are woven into the celebration of Word and Sacrament. This chapter gives special attention to cultivating values found in the early accounts of the Christian meal tradition, or communion. This survey points our own study of the relationship between Christians and care for the earth in two important directions: (1) identifying the central values that shape not just Eucharistic practice but the entire life of communities both within and outside of the church; and (2) examining how the values expressed in meal depictions in Scripture are embodied within the Christian tradition.

Hence, a first step that supports our journey to an eco-centric view of the universe is to listen to Scripture with an ear for the practices and values that animated early Christian communities. Our goal is not to attempt to simply recreate these practices in our twenty-first-century settings. Instead, we are looking at how the diverse practices of different communities supported Christian virtues that drew on a coherent vision of God's presence in all of creation. This survey of meal customs will help us to recover and highlight particular values that connect the participants to one another and to the world around them.

GETTING OUR HOUSE IN ORDER

As noted in chapter 2, Larry Rasmussen describes the need for the church to shift from an ego-centered to eco-centered view of the universe. Instead of placing ourselves at the center of the universe, we accept ourselves as part of the cosmos and assume our responsibility to care for the gift of creation and to live in light of God's presence and grace, which permeate the universe. In this work, the church has a calling to present a moral vision of shared life based on principles of ecological sustainability that support the needs of the planet and define our place in the ecosystem. Rasmussen presents this "vision of 'ecological civilization' as the alternative to industrial civilization."[2]

The transition to this new way of seeing ourselves in the world includes several important aspects. First, Christians must move away from the patterns of consumption imbedded in popular culture and the market-driven economy. The church is called to assume a countercultural witness that rejects the values of rampant consumerism. We must remind ourselves that responding to advertising by acquiring more stuff or the next great thing does not bring us happiness. Market philosophies based on greed and hoarding do not provide us comfort or decrease our anxiety.

In addition to helping members of both our congregations and the wider community shift away from constant consumption, which drains us of our energy and the earth of its resources, the church has the opportunity to provide a home that welcomes all to join us in practices that will sustain the earth. This vision draws on the language of *oikos*, the Greek word for *house* and *household*. This word is the root of the English words *ecology, ecumenism*, and *economy*.[3] These shared linguistic roots show us that there is an integral relationship between the way we live in the world (ecology), the way people of faith relate to one another (ecumenism, or the church's vision of our common faith), and the household rules for the well-being of our homes (economics, which includes stewardship of our financial resources as well as the earth's resources).[4] Reclaiming this vision of a sustainable life requires the church to exercise its voice and live out a holistic witness of life that holds these diverse pieces together. The church is called to demonstrate that how we relate to the world has a direct effect on how we interact with each other, including the economic rules, agreements, and practices we adopt for our own well-being, for the benefit of those around us, and for the good of the earth.

INFLUENCES ON OUR UNDERSTANDING AND PRACTICE OF THE EUCHARIST

The words that share the root *oikos* suggest that there were times in history when communities held together core values that supported the earth, households, and common faith. In places, these shared values affected Christians' understanding of humanity's place within the broader cosmos. Language about the grandeur of creation and God's providence as creator and provider marked the theology and practice of these Christian assemblies. Looking back at these times can help us discover ways to reclaim a more integrated vision of life. We can learn much by examining how the first followers of Jesus held these values together. What practices sustained the early church in its mission and ministry in a world that was often hostile to the message of the Gospel?

I believe the communal practices of eating together, as described in the Gospels and the book of Acts, are significant guides to help us integrate our theological beliefs and values with our daily lives. Note, this striking testimony from the earliest days of the church after Pentecost:

> They devoted themselves to the apostles' teaching and fellowship, to the breaking of bread and the prayers. Awe came upon everyone, because many wonders and signs were being done by the apostles. All who believed were together and had all things in common; they would sell their possessions and goods and distribute the proceeds to all, as any had need. Day by day, as they spent much time together in the Temple, they broke bread at home and ate their food with glad and generous hearts, praising God and having the goodwill of all the people. And day by day the Lord added to their number those who were being saved. (Acts 2:42–47).

The Spirit's coming to the first Christian believers at the harvest festival celebration of Pentecost led them to a communal way of life. The testimony of Christ's resurrection took hold in the lives of followers, who devoted themselves to the practices of prayer and breaking bread. Note the key elements that led to the church's growth:

1. The believers' devotion to the apostles' teaching and fellowship refers to their sharing the stories of Jesus's life and ministry and discovering ways to embody these accounts in the life of the community.

2. References to the prayers likely refer to their continued participation in the daily prayers offered at the Temple.
3. And the breaking of the bread is the standard language that Luke uses throughout the Gospel and the book of Acts to refer to communion practices.

This foundation (note the implication that this foundation consists of Word and Sacrament) emphasizes both the wonders and signs performed by the apostles as well as the growth and transformation of the community. The rapid expansion of this small core of believers is the outgrowth of the Spirit's prompting them to share what they had, so that no one would be in need. Acts 2 gives a clear picture of the connections between how we live together, care for one another and for the world, and create patterns that sustain our lives and help us to flourish.

We can gain more guidance, though, from this snapshot of the early church. How might our own Eucharistic practices draw on the descriptions of their practices? Answering this question requires us to peel back the assumptions about the origin and history of the Eucharist that we often bring to communion.

A close examination of our communion liturgies indicates that we rely primarily on accounts of the Last Supper. Our Eucharistic prayers are based almost exclusively on Luke's account of Jesus's last meal with his disciples in the Upper Room and on the apostle Paul's version of this narrative for the church in Corinth.[5] The "words of institution" are so central in our communion prayers that these are the only words required by some Protestant denominations.

The Gospels, though, include descriptions of numerous other shared meals in Jesus's public ministry as well as in the accounts of his resurrection appearances that often include Eucharistic imagery. For example, biblical and liturgical scholars have long recognized that Luke's language in both the Gospel and the book of Acts of Jesus taking, breaking, blessing, and giving bread are shorthand for Eucharistic practice. Rather than build on this four-fold pattern to encourage diverse prayers and practices, the church has followed a far narrower, restrictive approach in texts of Eucharistic prayers.

In the mid-twentieth century, the classic work of Dom Gregory Dix in *The Shape of the Liturgy* popularized the theory that Eucharistic prayer and practice have followed a particular form throughout history. Dix's thesis provided a historical and biblical rationale for preserving a particular form of communion prayers. A primary goal of celebrating the Lord's Supper was to continue the tradition, regardless of later historical and cultural influences.

Early Christian worship drew on a variety of local and cultural influences that shaped the way Christians gathered to tell stories and memories of Jesus and to share a common meal in their worship gatherings. Recent research on the origins of the Eucharist points to diverse practices that influenced ways that Christians gathered to break bread. Communities drew on their own unique cultural patterns to shape their worship. In particular, the work of Paul Bradshaw challenges the dominance of Dix's hypothesis: "So seductive has been the picture painted by Dix that it has tended to blind us to its shortcomings and thus mislead us."[6] Bradshaw asserts that there is no evidence that early Eucharistic meals followed the pattern of the Last Supper. Regular communion meals (note that in the Acts text, they broke bread daily) did not seek to replicate the ritual patterns and required food and drink of an annual Passover meal shared by Jesus and his disciples in the Upper Room in Jerusalem. Instead, the evidence suggests that early Christian meals relied on other resources for organizing their meal gatherings.

Bradshaw couples this sharp critique of the notion that the church has at all times and in all places followed a universal model of communion with an impressive demonstration of the diversity of meal practices in the early centuries of the Christian church. Eucharistic meals ran a wide gamut from full meals like the one described in 1 Corinthians 11, to simple meals of bread and water. Bradshaw cites evidence that communion meals included oil, bread, vegetables, salt, cheese, and milk and honey.[7] Diversity of practice, particularly in different geographic areas, was normative and valued. Communion in North Africa likely looked quite different from the gatherings in Antioch.

This diversity in practice lasted for four centuries in the Western church until the powers in Rome required conformity in the church's liturgy. In fact, it was not until 393 C.E. that the Synod of Hippo passed a rule that stipulated that only bread and wine mixed with water were allowed on the communion table.[8]

MEAL VALUES

In recent years, New Testament and liturgical scholars have shown how Greco-Roman banquets influenced Eucharistic practices. Examining the values that were a part of these meal gatherings will help us identify ways that these values can support us in caring for one another and for the earth. Recent studies of Greco-Roman banquet meals show that in the ancient world, banquets began with eating, followed by a time of drinking and conversation. Wide varieties of clubs, civic organizations, and religious groups, including Christians, used this widely accepted structure, adapting it in ways that supported their own philosophical interests and commitments.[9]

The work of several New Testament scholars shows how prominent aspects of this approach to banquets permeate the Gospels. In particular, the work of New Testament scholars Dennis Smith and Hal Taussig has strengthened our understanding of the diverse influences on the development of Eucharistic practices in the early Christian movement. [10] From the descriptions of reclining (a distinct posture of the banquet meals) to the discussions of seating arrangements, the Gospels show a familiarity with these ancient banquets. For our purposes, though, the significance of the specific ancient Greco-Roman eating practices lies in the values at the core of these meals, particularly the connection of these meals to Christian celebration of the earth as God's creation.

In analyzing the descriptions of the banquet tradition, New Testament scholar Matthias Klinghardt identifies three distinctive ideals expressed in the meal gatherings: community, equality, and good order. [11] A shared meal allowed participants to bond with one another. Group identity was formed by the time spent eating, drinking, and talking together. The sense of fellowship or *koinonia* grew out of the shared actions of those who gathered. The acts of eating the same food, drinking the same wine, and singing together were central in creating the sense of community that nurtured group identity. [12]

A second purpose of the banquet was to encourage feelings of equality among the participants. At times, accomplishing this goal was particularly challenging, since seating arrangements always implied a ranking system. (Consider our own seating arrangements at dinner parties and the importance of sitting near the head of the table.) Thus, hosts faced the difficult challenge of recognizing honored guests, while creating an atmosphere where all received equal treatment. The goal of this undertaking was to foster friendships based on feelings of mutual equality among those who had gathered. [13]

A third value of the meal tradition was to promote a sense of good order among the participants. Hosts held the significant responsibility of facilitating the dining, drinking, and conversation in ways that were lively and engaging, but yet did not allow guests to get out of control. On this point, Smith notes the development of certain rules of etiquette for those who were participating. [14]

These ideals guided participants in both civic and religious meal gatherings. For our purposes, though, we can look at how these ideals connect with Christian practices and help us integrate faith and life when Christians gather for worship. Scripture gives a clear example, albeit a negative one, of what is at stake when Christians gather to celebrate the Lord's Supper. In 1 Corinthians 11, the apostle Paul expresses to the church in Corinth his concern about the reports of their meal that he has received. Their practices are causing division within the church. Some individuals come to the banquet early, have lots to eat, and drink so much wine that they become drunk. Others, who arrive later, do not even get enough to eat. Because they did not share the same food and drink (and even ate and drank separately), and because of disorderly conduct, the goals of the banquet tradition that should have unified the assembly were nullified.

Note, though, that Paul's critique of the church's worship practices is not that the community failed to live up to the ideals of the Greco-Roman banquet. After all, Greek and Roman literature are filled with stories of banquets that went awry. Instead, for Christians the ideals of the banquet tradition were reappropriated to support the primary goal of building Christian faith. Paul cites the authority of Jesus in his strong rebuke of the Corinthians' practice.

Paul's description of Jesus sharing bread and cup with his disciples at the Last Supper provides a corrective pattern. Bread and wine are shared with all. Participants gather in memory of and thanksgiving for God's redemptive work freeing Israel from Egypt. The broader banquet values of community, equality, and good order are all affirmed by the meal in the Upper Room. Paul uses the narrative of the Last Supper as a way to focus these shared ideals on the task of building up the church and supporting the life of discipleship for those who gather. Paul invites the congregation in Corinth to examine their own practices to see if they are living out these shared values and focusing on their commitment to follow Jesus Christ.

In his investigation of Greco-Roman meals, Dennis Smith adds one additional value that is worth noting: a central aspect of the gatherings was to promote feelings of "festive joy." Enjoyment and pleasure are standard expectations for those who participate in the meals. The hope is that all participants will experience "good cheer" as a result of the activities.[15] Christian communities interpreted this goal in relationship to life in Christ. For example, note how the first Christians who gathered daily in their homes to break bread together are described as eating with glad and generous hearts (Acts 2:46). In contrast, Paul notes in 1 Corinthians 11 that because divisions are occurring, joy is not shared by all members of the community.

Christian meals followed the format and goals of the Greco-Roman banquets, including the emphasis on cultivating shared values of community, equality, good order, and joy. However, Christian gatherings applied these values to the broader purpose of supporting the community members' growth as disciples of Jesus Christ. These shared experiences around the table helped Christians integrate faith in Christ into their daily lives. In this way, the meals wove together values that guided the participants in their household, economic, and faith activities (once again demonstrating the significance of the shared root, of *oikos*).

VALUES FOR CREATION CARE

We have examined the way that meals among the early Christians supported and developed values rooted in the faith of the community. Now we turn our attention to ways that recovering these values supports a commitment to creation care. First, affirming and living out the values of community, equality, good order, and joy connects with the need for us to change our behavior in light of the environmental crisis we face. We discussed this transition previously in terms of a change from an ego-centered to eco-centered view of the universe.

People of all faiths (and no faith) can share a commitment to protect both the earth as our habitat and the life forms (including us!) that depend on it. Community (dependence on one another), equality (mutual respect), and good order (protecting the diversity of life) are values that can bring all people together. Christians can labor side by side with others in the hard work of cleaning up our parks and beaches, advocating for change to public policies, reducing our carbon footprint, and creating sustainable patterns of living that support the common good. Whether through participating in Earth Day projects or responding together to environmental disasters, Christians can share values and practices with others in support of the earth's health and our own well-being.

Leaders in other disciplines note the importance of advocating similar goals to guide our commitment to the earth. In their groundbreaking work on architectural design, William McDonough and Michael Braungart describe the transformation that is necessary in order for us to move to an ecologically sustainable way of life. In charting the dramatic shifts required for us and the planet to survive, the authors use language that is strikingly similar to that of the ideals prized in the Greco-Roman banquets. McDonough and Braungart call for finding a balanced approach to the environmental crisis, one that honors the ecological environment, supports the economy, and is equitable to all who are involved.[16] Once again, that Greek word *oikos*, *home*, serves as a focal point. This sustainable way of life requires us to recognize the earth as our home by balancing the need for economic growth with respect and fairness for the needs of the ecosystem. The authors call us to commit to the following values: (1) ecological sustainability; (2) respect; and (3) delight, celebration, and fun.[17] Ecological sustainability requires us to give high priority to the well-being of the community. Respect grows as we honor the inherent value of the ecosystem. Delight comes from finding pleasure in all that we make and use. Thus, a call to ecologically sustainable practices in the world of architecture and design is surprisingly parallel to the ideals we uncovered in the ancient banquet tradition. Design and architecture are one example of partners that the church can find on this journey of transformation. Together, we can learn to see the world in a new way and take up practices that will sustain the earth and all life around us.

FOOD FOR THOUGHT

While Christians will find allies and conversation partners as we develop a theology of creation care, we must always ground our work in Word and Sacrament (the marks of the church). Our theological commitments shape ways in which the shared values serve the primary goal of nurturing faith when we gather for worship. We are called to live out our baptismal vows as disciples of Jesus Christ. On this journey of faith, it is helpful to look at Scripture to see how these values are expressed in the life of Jesus.

Descriptions of shared meals are prominent in the Gospels' portrait of Jesus's ministry. These accounts include conflicts over meal practices, parables, and reports of resurrection appearances. Throughout the Gospels, Jesus's practice of sharing meals embodies the ideals and values of community, equality, and good order, as well as creating occasions for festive joy. Consider the feeding of the 5,000. Luke 9:10–17 describes a crowd of people who surround Jesus in hopes of receiving healing and hearing his teaching. Near the end of the day, the disciples come to Jesus to request that he dismiss the crowd in order that the people might provide for themselves. However, Jesus responds by inviting the disciples to trust in the sufficiency of God's provision. In order to demonstrate that God sustains us, Jesus shuns the idea that the people rely on themselves. He asks the disciples to organize the mass of people in groups of fifty. Then, holding five loaves and two fish, he looks to heaven, invokes God's blessing, breaks the bread, and begins to share the meal with all. A common meal, available to all, becomes an occasion of proclaiming and embodying the good news of God's reign. Values imbedded in ways of eating bear witness to God's presence, which creates and sustain us.

Luke 14 provides an example of conflict in a meal setting portrayed in the Gospels. Jesus participates in a meal gathering at the home of a leader of the Pharisees. Jesus observes the guests jockeying to sit in positions of honor near the head of the table. This violation of the ideals of meal practices prompts Jesus to offer an alternative vision of life together. Rather than struggling to achieve prominent positions (an ego-centered approach), try a different practice, he advises. If you are invited to a wedding, pick out a place in the back of the room. Then, if you are asked to change seats, you will find yourself moving closer to the center of the celebration rather than away from it. Or, if you are serving as the host of a banquet, consider creating a guest list in an entirely different way. Rather than invite those who can return the favor, invite those who live on the margins of society: the poor, the crippled, the lame, and the blind. Practicing hospitality to those who cannot return it exemplifies a primary value for people of faith.

Just in case we miss the point, Jesus tells us a story: Once upon a time a prominent host was preparing a great banquet. He got everything prepared for this grand celebration and sent out his servants to notify guests that the evening's festivities were ready to commence. The guests, however, sent back word that they were busy with other activities: making real estate deals, buying livestock, setting up households. In the face of this rejection, the host sent out word to the poor and the forgotten to join him in this banquet. Thus, a new community was formed that was based not on reciprocity, but on generosity and hospitality.

The story of Zacchaeus in Luke 19 provides another example of these values. Here, the call to discipleship begins with Jesus's invitation to share a meal. Zacchaeus, a wealthy tax collector, climbs a tree to see Jesus as he enters Jericho. When Jesus sees the man, he calls out to him and declares that he is going to his house to eat with him. The crowd, who views Zacchaeus as a sinner unworthy of Jesus's time and attention, is shocked that Jesus intends to go stay with this man. Zacchaeus, though, recognizes this meeting as an opportunity to change his life. And indeed, Zacchaeus responds to the invitation: "Lord, I will give half of my possessions to the poor and will provide restitution to anyone whom I have cheated." In this encounter, an invitation to dine creates community, equality, and a new sense of order.

Similarly, notice how the Gospel of John portrays Jesus's actions at a wedding in Cana. Jesus turns the water into wine at this celebration as his first public sign, performed to reveal his glory and so that the disciples might believe (John 2:11). The Gospel takes care to place this first miracle in a public setting immediately preceding Jesus's cleansing of the Temple. The divine presence is revealed first at a gathering in the world and only later in the Temple. Again, the ideals of community, equality, good order (where Jesus provides for the wedding celebration to run its course), and festive joy are central to the narrative.

The Gospels' meal stories include two resurrection appearances with similar emphases. The meal following the encounter on the road to Emmaus in Luke 24 and the barbeque at the beach in John 21 both stress that gathering around a meal is central to the lives of Jesus's followers. Luke portrays the turning point in the story as the moment when Jesus takes bread and blesses, breaks, and gives it to the disciples (following the usual Eucharistic formula in Luke). Then they recognized the stranger as the risen Christ. In John 21, a stranger on the beach instructs the disciples, who had been fishing all night, to cast their nets on the other side of the boat. The miraculous haul of fish leads Peter to recognize the stranger as the risen Christ. The disciples join him around the fire for a shared meal. In resurrection life, we live out values around a table. Our lives as disciples of Christ come to embody community, equality, good order, and festive joy.[18]

Scripture, then, offers us models that encourage Christian communities to share a faith journey in ways that are just and sustainable. The earth and its goodness are often portrayed as signs of God's presence throughout the

Bible. Even when we may least expect to find God, Scripture presents portraits of this new way of life, which we are invited to discover and called to share. In these meal stories from the Gospels and the book of Acts, we have uncovered a set of values shared by the ancient world that can guide us in our growth as communities of faith today. These texts can serve as guides to help us find our way on this journey, while also grounding us in our identity as followers of Jesus Christ. Why not place these stories at the center of our own gatherings? Why not allow their language and values to infuse our own prayers and practices? Why not open ourselves and our worship services to make room for the earth and for each other, so that we will discover the presence of God in our midst?

As a start on this journey, the Eucharistic prayers scattered throughout this book infuse the memories of these shared meals into the seasons the church celebrates throughout the year. We gather at the table to celebrate the gift of life created by God, incarnate in Christ, enlivened by the Spirit. These prayers seek to expand both our memory and our imagination beyond a dark night long ago in an upper room, because the story that we share is not primarily one framed by Jesus's betrayal. Instead, the story is one of redemption that is woven throughout creation. It is a story that invites us to participate in God's ongoing redemptive work in our lives and throughout the world.

CONCLUSION

The task of learning to see the world around us and to live in it differently requires us to change the ways that we act both inside and outside our churches. As we saw, the values of forming community, practicing equality, creating good order, and experiencing festive joy took on a particular form in the Christian community. The cultural ideals of the banquet tradition were attached to specific goals within early Christian communities. While Christians adopted the gathering patterns for their meals from the culture around them, they adapted them to support their primary aim of shaping their lives in the likeness of Jesus Christ.

Christian practices around the ancient world provide us with inspiration and permission to explore faithful ways for us to gather in our communities. Releasing ourselves from prescriptive readings that restrict our interactions with one another and with the world makes room for the Spirit to breathe new life into our congregations and open up our worship practices to more fully celebrate the richness of creation and our place within it.

In this time of transformation, we will discover new partners who share our hopes of finding ways to live responsibly and to care for the planet. In this work, we will also learn to listen to our own sacred stories with a new ear and to hear ways that God continues to call us to tend the earth, provide for the poor, and care for the neglected and forgotten. In this task, we can renew and reform the rituals that have sustained the church throughout its history. As we focus on gathering around the table to share a meal, we have the opportunity to expand our practices to include other testimonies from Scripture that model ways for us to live faithfully as disciples of Jesus Christ. Their persistent call to us gives us a chance to get our house (*oikos*) in order.

Liturgical Resources

EPIPHANY

This is the message that we proclaim: God is light.
Let us walk in the light of God.
This is the hope that we share: that we have fellowship with Christ and one another.
Let us live together in joy and hope.

Prayer of the Day

God of all creation, the glory of your star pierces our darkness
    and illumines every corner of our lives.
Grant us so to live in your resplendent light
    that we may reflect your glory into all of creation,
    chasing the terrors of darkness from your world
    and restoring and refreshing all life on this planet that you created.
We pray with all of creation through Jesus Christ our Lord,
    who lives and reigns over all creation with you, in the power of the Holy Spirit,
    Three in One, One in Three, now and forever.
Amen.

Confession and Pardon

Hear these words of Scripture: "The light shines in the darkness and the darkness did not overcome it."
Let us turn from the ways of darkness and embrace the light.
Together, let us confess our sin to God and to another:

God of light and life,
You created us in your image to care for one another and for all of creation.
Forgive us for turning away from you, embracing the darkness, and ignoring the needs of our neighbor and the cries of the earth.
As the sun brings light and warmth to this earth, make us signs of your grace, through Christ, our light and life, we pray. Amen.

In the water of baptism, God's blessing is poured out upon us. All creation declares the goodness of God. May the light of Christ shine in our lives so that all may see God's glory. May we share this blessing as we care for others and for the earth so that all creation will declare God's glory.

Prayer for Illumination

God of light, shine your wisdom upon us today. As we hear your word, may we together discover your call to bring renewal to this world that you created and which you love. Amen.

Prayer of Dedication

Bless us, God, and these gifts that we bring that together we may share the light that you bring into this world. We ask this in the name of Christ, your gift to us. Amen.

EPIPHANY EUCHARIST

Scripture: Meal images from John 1 and the wedding at Cana (John 2)

Invitation to the Table

Hear these words of Scripture:
The true light, which enlightens everyone,
Is coming into the world.
And this Word became flesh and lived among us,
And we have seen the glory
Of the one who brings us grace and truth.
All those who long for the light are welcome at this table.

The Lord be with you.
And also with you.
Lift up your hearts.
We lift them up to the Lord.
Let us give thanks to God.
It is good to give our thanks and praise.

Creating God, in the beginning,
You created the heavens and the earth.
You separated the water from the land
And declared that it was good.
When we turned away from the light, you called us back with prophets who spoke your truth.
When we drank from other wells, you sent Jesus to call us back to the water that gives us eternal life.
So we join our voices with all of creation as it praises you:

Holy, holy, holy Lord,
God of power and might.
Heaven and earth are full of your glory.
Hosanna in the highest.
Blessed is the one who comes in the name of the Lord.
Hosanna in the highest.

We speak of your glory and we give thanks for the many ways that Christ is shown to us.
When Jesus entered the Jordan River to be baptized by John,
All creation was blessed.
At a wedding in Cana, Jesus transformed water into a wine as a sign of God's glory.
Here, your Word is revealed for all to taste and see,
And so that all may believe.

* * *

Remembering your glory shown to us in Jesus Christ
We take this bread made from the grain that grows up out of the earth
And this wine made from grapes that flourish in the sun
To celebrate your presence that sustains us as your children.
We offer ourselves that we too may be signs of your glory.

Great is the mystery of faith:
Christ has died.
Christ is risen.
Christ will come again.

Pour out your Spirit on us
And on this bread and cup
That here your glory may be revealed to us
And that, as your disciples, we too may believe.
Make us signs of your presence that others
May thirst for the grace that comes from you.
Show us ways to care for the earth that you created and placed us in.
Strengthen us to work for a world
where hunger and thirst will be no more.
Bind us together as a sign of presence in our world that we may glorify you,
Creator, Christ, and Spirit.
Amen.

The Lord's Prayer
Breaking of the Bread

When Jesus and his disciples gathered
    He took the cup and invited them to drink
    That they might know of God's glory.
Brothers and Sisters in Christ:
    Taste and see that God is good.

Chapter Four

A Baptismal Way of Life

Our survey of how the Gospels portray the ideals of meal gatherings showed how early Christian communities used these values in forming faithful disciples. The ideals of community, equality, good order, and festive joy took shape within the community as followers of Jesus gathered around the table to break bread and share a common cup. In these gatherings, they told stories and memories of Jesus's life and teaching and held open conversations about how to live into this new life together. These first Christians adopted a common way of signifying their commitment to the community: baptism.

Baptism as a unifying Christian initiation practice draws its clearest biblical precedent from Jesus's baptism in the Jordan River by John the Baptist. Each of the Gospels provides an account of this event, all presenting it as a defining moment in Jesus's ministry. His baptism is linked to his discernment and formation of his vocational identity, which leads to the beginning of his public ministry. In Matthew's Gospel, the movement is clear: Jesus joins the crowds in the wilderness who are responding to John's message of repentance and preparation for the coming of God's reign. The Gospels portray these events in the wilderness, in distinct contrast to Jerusalem, where the Temple stood at the center of power in Jewish life. The religious leaders join the crowd in journeying out to the wilderness to see and hear this prophetic figure.

John's role as the new Elijah is indicated by his emulation of the older prophet's attire: a signature wardrobe of camel's hair with a leather belt around his waist (Matthew 3:4). His diet of locusts and wild honey reinforces his association with the great Jewish prophet. Significant connections with other biblical events are clearly intended. Following forty years of wandering in the wilderness, the Hebrews made their way through the Jordan River to enter the promised land. This water crossing was in itself a recurrence of their crossing through the Red Sea in their exodus from slavery in Egypt. Jewish hearers of this text would quickly have picked up on these familiar themes. Linking these faith stories from the past to the present day conditions was a central part of reform movements in first-century Judaism.

The crowd responds to John's prophetic call by entering the Jordan River, confessing their sins, and being baptized. Jesus responds to this call to renewal by presenting himself to be baptized by John. Matthew's explanatory notes suggest his struggle to find an explanation for Jesus's participation in this event. John declares he is unworthy to baptize Jesus, but Jesus insists that his baptism is to fulfill Scripture. The baptism includes the heavens opening, a dove descending, and a divine voice pronouncing, "This is my Son, the beloved, with whom I am well pleased" (Matthew 3:17).

Each of these actions further deepens the narrative ties to significant texts in the Hebrew Scriptures.[1] Immediately following Jesus's baptism comes a forty-day period of testing in the wilderness, where Jesus struggles to find a way to live out this divine calling.[2] This period of discernment marks Jesus's preparation for beginning his public ministry by calling the first disciples.

The early church seized on this baptismal narrative in spite of any concerns that they had regarding connections between baptism and Jewish reform movements. John's Gospel takes care to underscore that Jesus himself did not baptize, even though some of his disciples may have been involved in John's ministry (John 3). Judaism's practice of baptism as an act of cleansing and renewal was picked up by other groups. For example, Jewish Essenes practiced ritual water cleansings. Other religious groups, including some Greek and Roman mystery religions, also used water in their own rites of initiation. Any similarities between John's baptism and other groups' practices failed to deter Jesus's followers from quickly adapting this ritual for their own purposes.[3]

What prompted early Jewish Christians to adopt baptism as a defining act of inclusion into the community? Perhaps the power of the stories of Jesus's baptism inspired them to interpret their own baptism in light of these accounts. In their desire to identify with Christ, they discovered a strong connection between the presence of the Spirit associated with Jesus's baptism, and their own vocational discernment. Their call to follow Jesus prompted them to take on the signs of Christ's ministry, beginning with his baptism.

These followers of Jesus interpreted baptism as an act in which they took on the pattern of Jesus's life. The apostle Paul provided the clearest Christological interpretation of baptism in his epistle to the church in Rome: "Do you not know that all of us who have been baptized into Christ Jesus were baptized into his death? Therefore we have been buried with him by baptism into death, so that, just as Christ was raised from the dead by the glory of the Father, so we too might walk in newness of life" (Romans 6:3–4). For Paul, the baptismal act of mimesis and repetition goes beyond the simple narrative of Jesus's baptism and is extended into the cruciform shape of Christ's life, which ends on a cross. Baptism, then, is participation in Jesus's life, death, and resurrection. The Gospel takes shape in our own lives as we are submerged in the water and raised again to a new life.

In the process of adapting Jewish practices of ritual cleansing, the early church made significant changes to the ritual. Baptism became a one-time event rather than an ongoing process of purification.[4] Christians looked at their own baptisms through multiple stories of Jesus's baptism and the community's growing theological interpretation of baptism as an act of solidarity with Jesus's ministry. A commitment to Christian discipleship became integrally connected to the meanings and patterns of baptism. Throughout the book of Acts, the decision to follow Jesus is linked with baptism. From the initial response to Peter's sermon on Pentecost (where 3,000 are baptized) to Christianity's growth among the Gentiles, baptism becomes the central, required act for those who join the Jesus movement.

While the first Christians reached a consensus that baptism marks one as a follower of Jesus, they remained flexible about the ritual dimensions of baptism. The New Testament includes a variety of images, formulas, and patterns for baptism. Christian baptism was influenced by the ritual practices of other religious traditions as well as from Roman bathing customs. As with communion, Christians adapted ritual elements from surrounding cultures in diverse ways.

There is a growing recognition among scholars that as the Christian movement spread across the Roman Empire, baptismal practice took on unique features of local communities. Liturgical scholar Bryan Spinks concludes his analysis of the documents from the first three centuries, "The different ritual patterns found in the early Christian evidences mirror secular bathing customs."[5] For example, some Christian communities used incense; others, ritual lamps and torches. Anointing before and/or after bathing quickly became a customary part of baptism. Local communities of Christians, however, likely followed regional, cultural habits in their choices about when to anoint the individual and in other actions associated with bathing customs that became part of the baptismal liturgy. Over time these ritual elements were given theological interpretations. For example, oil's use for sealing and preservation is interpreted as the Spirit's work of redeeming us, and a lighted candle is for illumination, just as Christ's light leads us out of darkness. After surveying the biblical images of baptism, Spinks concludes, "The New Testament is both the fulcrum from which emerges all theological reflection on baptism and all Christian baptismal rites, and the touchstone, or "norming norm" against which they may be tested. However, the books of the New Testament present neither a single doctrine of baptism, nor some archetypal liturgical rite."[6] Scripture serves as a guide in helping us discern ways that the early church filled out and interpreted the ritual of baptism and its relationship to Christian discipleship.

BACK TO NATURE

Our interest in baptism includes ways that this practice relates to creation care. An aspect of Jesus's baptism that we often overlook is that it takes place in nature. The Jewish institutional practice of ritual cleansing at the Temple (observant Jews bathed in pools called *mikveh* baths) is set aside, and Jesus and his followers are immersed in a river, understood as a source of renewal. While there are theological motives for locating the baptisms in the Jordan River, other baptismal stories take place in natural settings as well. Consider the account of Philip and the Ethiopian eunuch in Acts 8. The text notes that the eunuch is returning to his home after traveling to worship at the Temple in Jerusalem. Here is the portrait of a man so devout that he studies Scripture as he travels. Philip's interpretation of the Isaiah text leads the eunuch to a moment of decision. "Look, here is water," he proclaims as they come up to a pool of water. "What is to prevent me from being baptized?" So Philip and the man "went down into the water," where he was baptized (Acts 9:37–38). Water and word called out to him and prompted his response to the good news about Jesus.

The early church maintained a strong preference for the use of running water (instead of collected water) in their baptisms. In the *Didache*, an early commentary on Christian practices, the following instructions on baptism are offered:

> Now about baptism: this is how to baptize. Give public instruction on all these points, and then "baptize" in running water, "in the name of the Father and of the Son and of the Holy Spirit." If you do not have running water, baptize in some other. If you cannot in cold, then in warm. If you have neither, then pour water on the head three times "in the name of the Father, Son, and Holy Spirit."[7]

Running water in a natural setting was preferred for baptisms. Nature was recognized as an appropriate site for celebrating one's new life as a disciple of Jesus Christ. Theologian Linda Gibler observes that *The Apostolic Tradition of Hippolytus*, another early work that includes instructions for baptism, similarly suggests that baptismal candidates visit the water where they will be baptized and offer a prayer over it in hopes that the water will be "pure and flowing" at the time of their baptism. This leads Gibler to conclude: "For at least the first two hundred years of Christian tradition water was not blessed for baptism. Clean, living water did not need to be blessed."[8]

The difference between using living water and collected (stale) water in baptism leads Gibler to explore the ways that running water supports life. Building on the creation stories in Genesis, she notes the primary role of water in supporting the forms of life on earth: "After being formed by stars and assisting in their birth, water was ready to midwife life on Earth."[9] Water, as it is found in nature, is a central part of birth and new life.

Baptism by immersion into the earth's natural water is a clear reminder of our connection to creation. In the story of Jesus's baptism, the early church fathers saw a way of strengthening these ties. When Jesus entered the water of the Jordan River, all of creation was blessed by his presence. Melito of Sardis, a second-century bishop, describes Jesus's baptism as part of a "universal baptism" in which all creation participates. "Should it be a matter of surprise that Christ, the king of heaven and creation's captain, a Sun out of heaven, should be bathed in the Jordan?"[10] Jesus participates in the act of baptism as a way of sanctifying the baptismal way of life that runs through the course of nature. The renewal of the earth depends on the gift of water that sustains life. Living water brings forth, nurtures, and sustains life. Baptism is a way of participating in this elemental aspect of life.

For Christians in the twenty-first century to capture the significance of this process of renewal, we will need to stop taking water for granted in our daily lives. From the moment we rise each morning and step into the bathroom to take a shower; to the times we pause to drink the water that our bodies depend on; to the evening, when we wash our faces and brush our teeth, we rely on access to clean, potable water. We are surrounded by water in oceans, lakes, or rivers that supports life on earth. Our bodies and the earth are made up largely of water, and we rely on it to sustain our lives. In cultures and times when humans walk long distances to carry water for their own use, people readily understand water as a precious commodity. Easy access to water in our homes, however, reinforces the tendency for us simply to take it for granted.

Water's basic role in life led communities to use it in rituals as well. It is not surprising that nearly all religions use water as a part of their rituals. The church gravitated to baptism—using water, a primary gift of God's work of creation—as a way to enact our response to God's call to discipleship. Ethicist John Hart suggests that there is a close tie between the ability of water to evoke images of cleansing and new life in baptismal rites and the availability of clean water in the world around us. Polluted water lacks the power to embody the ritual claims of God's grace that we celebrate in baptism. The loss of clean, available water carries with it significant consequences for our daily lives as well as our rituals.

> Throughout the world today . . . environmental degradation and water privatization have caused water to lose its nature and role as living water, as a

> bountiful source of benefits for the common good. Water is losing also its
> ability to be a sacramental symbol, a sign in nature of God the Creator. [11]

An important benefit of having water in the baptisteries and fonts in our sanctuaries is that its presence prompts us to consider the basic contributions of water to our lives each day. All water carries a sacred dimension, since life depends upon it. Or, as Gibler observes, water is not only a "symbol of grace," it is "fecund with grace in its own right."[12] Running water, clean and available to all, serves as a sign of God's goodness in creating and sustaining life in the universe. When we use water in our religious rituals, we are echoing the claim that God provides for our needs and welcomes us to care for creation.

Baptism, then, weaves together the two central strands of our study: discipleship and creation. Christians use water as a way to ritually embody our call to follow Jesus Christ. Drawing on the story of Jesus's baptism and the patterns of Scripture and the early church, baptism serves as a defining mark in celebrating our response to God's grace. At the same time, the physical act of baptism with water, used generously and abundantly, immerses our bodies in this basic element of creation.

Congregational leaders seeking renewal by focusing on creation care find a natural starting place in the sacrament of baptism. With this act, we acknowledge our dependence on God, who provides the gift of water that we use to mark ourselves as disciples of Jesus Christ. The call to follow Christ is also a call to care for this creation, a gift from God. To grow into this life of discipleship is to care for one another and the signs of God's presence in the world, which include the water that runs down our foreheads.

Baptism is a lifelong journey of faith and not simply a momentary event. Many congregations are rediscovering that baptismal preparation and post-baptismal formation are significant ways to nurture people as they grow into Christian faith. Recovering the process of preparing candidates for baptism, often referred to as the *catechumenate*, provides a pattern for forming disciples by adapting practices from the early centuries of the church to our own time and settings.[13] Including creation care as part of this process of formation will deepen and strengthen the church's witness to caring for the earth as a central part of our faith journey. This kind of preparation for discipleship guides people to experience new life in a community that works for the well-being of all creation. Part of the process of nurturing disciples should include helping people discover gifts for service and opportunities to promote the earth's healing.

RENEWING THIS COMMITMENT

Linking our baptismal lives with care for creation can include regularly renewing our baptismal vows in a service that also gives special attention to the
needs of the world around us. Services for baptismal renewal are particularly
appropriate at designated times during the liturgical year, such as Baptism of
the Lord, or as part of an Easter Vigil. Another option for heightening the
connections between discipleship and creation care is to include a time for a
renewal of baptism during a special service focused on the needs of creation
(for example, as part of an ecumenical Earth Day service). A recent ecumenical resource from Scotland (prepared for use by Roman Catholics and Presbyterians) provides a prayer for the renewal of baptismal vows in light of the
need to care for creation. The liturgy includes the following affirmation,
"Commitment to the Christian Life":

> As a disciple of Christ will you continue
> in the Apostles' teaching and fellowship,
> in the breaking of bread
> and in prayer?
> **With the help of God, I will.**
> Will you proclaim the good news by word and deed,
> serving Christ in all people?
> **With the help of God, I will.**
> Will you work for justice and peace,
> honoring God in all creation?
> **With the help of God, I will.**
> This is the task of the Church.
> **This is our task;**
> **to live and work for the kingdom of God.** [14]

This liturgy uses strong language to claim that in caring for the earth we are
honoring God and working toward the coming of God's reign. The call to
live as disciples of Jesus Christ *is* a call to work for the renewal of the earth.
The liturgy can be strengthened by inviting brief testimonies from members
of the congregation. Individuals can give examples of ways in which they see
their work to care for the earth as part of their ministry as a follower of
Christ.

SEEKING CONGREGATIONAL CHANGE

Incorporating creation care into our liturgies and the lives of our communities is a gradual process. Congregational change often starts slowly. Efforts
to promote creation care practices in the life of First Presbyterian Church in
Newport, Oregon, began with just two committed people. Barrie and Denise

decided to work on small issues, such as replacing Styrofoam cups, which are bad for the environment, with reusable mugs at the community coffee hour each Sunday. Serving fair-trade coffee was next on the agenda. They eventually asked their pastor if they could start a committee on eco-spiritual-ity. The work of the committee expanded to address conservation issues for the church building, explore the use of church property for a community garden, acquire eco-theological resources for the church library, purchase greener resources for the church kitchen and fellowship times, and sponsor occasional worship services that highlight ecological themes.

An important value that guides the work of earth care centers on living out faith in the context of a community. Frequently individuals in congrega-tions are already active in environmental practices and movements. By start-ing an eco-justice group and inviting others into the process, Barrie and Denise created space for people with a shared passion to come together to work for the common good. Moving beyond individual actions to discern communal values and practices takes time, energy, and commitment, and success and setbacks have both been part of the process.

In a congregational context, pastors can help nurture individuals in their attempt to invite others to join in this work. Members of the eco-justice committee in Newport talked to me about the importance of relating to other committees and groups in the church, especially the church's session, the governing board that makes decisions for the congregation. They now have representatives who serve on that committee board. They found that it was critical to have representatives on the church's primary committees, especial-ly when facing significant decisions, such as adding solar panels or a wind generator for their primary energy source.

Changes of this nature often come slowly, and individual congregations will move at their own pace in light of particular priorities. Transforming the culture of an institution requires patience and flexibility. Listening to mem-bers articulate needs and possibilities is an important starting point in this process. Ethicist Larry Rasmussen notes the importance of addressing partic-ular concerns in facilitating this work:

> This means that spiritual-moral formation is irreducibly concrete and local, even when it is formation of a shared Earth ethic. It happens person by person, congregation by congregation, institution by institution, system by system. And it happens by way of multiple points of entry and multiple means as expressed by the whole people of God—young and old, lettered and unlet-tered, male and female, of whatever race, class, nationality or ecclesial tradi-tion.[15]

Pastors can play a central role in transforming the culture of congregations by encouraging members to step forward and claim leadership roles. Change will be more lasting and effective when ideas and initiatives come from members of the congregation. Online resources like webofcreation.org provide helpful suggestions about starting an eco-justice group in your congregation.[16] Many denominations also have national staff and resources to support the work of greening your congregation.

Another helpful starting point for the formation of a new creation care group is to invite members to look closely at the congregation's current practices. Eco-justice groups can play an important role in helping to hold congregations accountable for their actions. A group might ask: Is our congregation using pesticides so the church lawn looks green? Have we looked for ways to reduce our level of energy consumption? It is not enough for the preacher to wax eloquent in sermons about the importance of caring for the earth. A high level of commitment and action is required by the community of faith to live out the Gospel in ways that show our love of the earth. Without tangible results, congregations reinforce a prevailing notion held by many outside the church that Christians are hypocrites, because we often talk one way and live another way.

Our baptismal calling demands that we respond to the seriousness of the environmental crisis that the earth faces. As we work to change our habits and support the earth's healing, Christians must also recognize that we cannot solve these problems on our own. Rasmussen helpfully describes the process of working for change as the creation of "anticipatory communities," groups that lean into the future together. He explains, "Anticipatory communities initially come about voluntarily: hearts, minds, and the perception of what is 'real' are vital elements."[17] Thus, eco-justice groups work as yeast within the life of a congregation to help grow a deeper, lasting commitment to the work of caring for the earth. They are made up of members of the community who see the need for change and who come together in order to help transformation take shape in our congregations. They serve, Rasmussen says, as "home places where it is possible to reimagine worlds and reorder possibilities, places where new or renewed practices give focus to an ecological and postindustrial way of life."[18]

Once again, pastors and congregational leaders can play a critical role by creating a supportive environment in which this work takes place. Undergirding the work of these groups with theological reflections and grounding their practices in prayer and discernment allows groups to emerge as more than interest groups or "those environmentally minded (green) folks." Effective leaders look for ways to deepen the theological and spiritual foundation of those who step forward to lead the congregation in adopting creation care practices. Simple steps include welcoming and promoting the emergence of an eco-justice group in the church newsletter and acknowledging their work in a sermon.

Congregational transformation that is embedded in the worship life of the church and the celebration of the sacraments provides a fertile ground for communities of faith to grow and blossom in the work of linking discipleship and creation care. For change to take hold at the center of congregational life, pastors will need to show how this work of creation care relates to the church's commitment to Word and Sacrament.

SEEKING BAPTISMAL LINKS

A first step in this integration process is to acknowledge the work of the eco-justice committee and ask God's blessings on the members of this group during a Sunday morning service. Gathering around the font to celebrate the work of this committee connects the sacrament of baptism with the work of creation care and shows worshipers that this initiative is grounded in the call to Christian discipleship. Here is another opportunity to reinforce the theological conviction that baptism is a lifelong journey that requires leadership and support as members of the committee help us discover just and sustainable practices. Consider inviting committee members, if not the entire congregation, to gather around the font, then pour water in the font, while reading an appropriate biblical text, such as the following:

> They shall build houses and inhabit them;
>> they shall plant vineyards and eat their fruit.
> They shall not build and another inhabit;
>> they shall not plant and another eat;
> for like the days of a tree shall the days of my people be,
>> and my chosen shall long enjoy the work of their hands.
> The wolf and the lamb shall feed together,
>> the lion shall eat straw like the ox;
>> but the serpent—its food shall be dust!
> They shall not hurt or destroy
>> on all my holy mountain, says the Lord. (Isaiah 65:21–25)

Following the Scripture reading, offer a prayer of dedication for the group's work to bless and honor the commitment of these members of the congregation. This prayer provides a powerful, public witness to the congregation that the work of this committee is not simply on the periphery of the church's life, but that it is integral to the calling that we all share to join in God's redemptive work in the world.

Beyond the dedication of an eco-justice committee, I urge congregations to consider taking a further step by designating and commissioning church members with particular skills and talents (such as conservation advocates or gardeners) to serve as Earth Stewards. In this act, the congregation identifies, recognizes, and prays for particular individuals who model central values of creation care in the life of the congregation. In addition, the worshiping congregation lifts up and celebrates these values and connects them to the sacramental life of the community. Consider doing this as part of a special service that focuses on creation care. For example, if your congregation includes an Earth Day service, you may want to add a time for commissioning as a way of showing how the ongoing work of creation care in your congregation relates to an annual or occasional service. The goal here is to build on occasional services by connecting them to the ongoing work of creation care.

A worship service to commission Earth Stewards might include the following ritual:

Leader: Today, we gather around the baptismal font to recognize those whose gifts show us ways to care for the earth and to provide for our neighbors. Hear these words of Scripture: *(Leader pours water into the font.)*
"We know that the whole creation has been groaning in labor pains until now; and not only the creation, but we ourselves, who have the first fruits of the Spirit, groan inwardly while we wait for adoption, the redemption of our bodies. For in hope we were saved." (Romans 8:22–24)
In our baptism, "we are called by God to be the church of Jesus Christ, a sign in the world today of what God intends for all humankind." [19]
N. and N.,
as you live out your baptismal promises,
will you care for the goodness of creation and show us ways to preserve the signs of God's presence among us?
Earth Stewards: We will, with God's help.
Will you welcome others to join you in this ministry?
Earth Stewards: We welcome all to join us.
Laying on of hands: All are invited to lay hands on those being commissioned as a sign of blessing. [20]
Leader: Creating God, pour out your Spirit
on these whose ministry leads us in ways to see the goodness of your creation
and to care for the world around us.
Give them strength to work for the renewal
that you are bringing to the earth.
Guide them to discover ways to invite all people
to find your presence in the world around us
and respond by caring for creation.
We ask this in the name of Jesus Christ,
the first-born of creation. Amen.

"Whatever you do, in word or deed, do everything in the name of the Lord Jesus, giving thanks to God through him." (Colossians 3:17)
Passing of the Peace

Once again, worship is the primary place in which we gather to hear and respond to the Gospel's call to love God with all our heart, mind, and soul and love our neighbor as ourselves. By recognizing those who connect their gifts for service to the needs of the earth, congregations nurture members who will provide leadership as we work for the earth's renewal.

CONCLUSION

Grounding creation care in our baptismal calling provides us with a theological vision for our actions. Identifying individuals' gifts for responding to the earth's needs as a part of their own Christian vocation allows us the opportunity to ground these commitments in baptism. Supporting the work of an eco-justice group and honoring their commitment to service as they gather around a baptismal font extends the lines of our baptismal theology from a moment in time to a lifetime calling. When we identify members who will lead the congregation's commitment to earth care, we embody a baptismal theology that exemplifies our common commitment to a priesthood of all believers. In this process, effective leaders recognize practices of creation care and connect them with the liturgical life of the church as a way of witnessing to the Spirit's work among us. Sacramental renewal and caring for the earth provide complementary ways of breathing new life into our communities of faith. As we celebrate God's work of redemption with the earth's gifts of water, bread, and wine, we pledge to care for one another, the environment, and all of creation.

Liturgical Resources

LENT

For forty days, Jesus went into the wilderness to discern God's call.
For forty days, we prepare ourselves to mark the events of Holy Week.
May God's Spirit accompany us as we seek to discover God's call.
Let us worship God who leads us through the wilderness.

Prayer of the Day

Creator God, whose Son faced temptation forty days in the wilderness,
teach us how to live in such unity with you and your world
    that we may also refuse those temptations that we face.
Grant us grace to so order our lives, living as members of your good created
world, that all creation may well thrive in good measure, without want or fear
of want.
We pray for these gifts through Jesus Christ our Lord,
    who lives and reigns over all creation with you, in the power of the Holy
Spirit, Three in One, One in Three, now and forever.
Amen.

Confession and Pardon

We live in a world filled with pain and brokenness where creation groans with
us and calls out for God's healing. God will not abandon us, but calls us to
acknowledge our dependence on grace for each and every breath of life. In
faith, let us confess our sin to God and to one another:

**Generous God, we confess that we grow weary of working for peace and
justice for our neighbors and for all of creation. Forgive us when we
choose the easy path rather than follow your call on the journey that leads
to the cross. Give us your strength and your companionship that we may
be faithful disciples and work for the healing of the world, through Christ
we pray. Amen.**

In the midst of brokenness, God brings healing and wholeness.
In the midst of despair, God brings hope.
In the face of death, God brings us new life.
The risen Christ meets us here and leads us on our journey.
Know that you are forgiven and live in peace.

Chapter 4

Prayer for Illumination

Send your Spirit on us, O God, so that as we hear your word we will respond to your call to live as faithful discipleship to care for the earth and for one another; through Christ we pray. Amen.

Prayer of Dedication

Generous God, receive our gifts. Bless them and us that we may be signs of your presence in this world that you created and which you love. Amen.

LENT EUCHARIST

Scripture: Meal images from John 21

Come, all who long for signs of new life.
Come, those who have turned away or retreated to the past.
Come, those who are discouraged and have lost hope.
Here at this table, as we break bread and share it with one another,
The risen Christ meets us to feed us and lead us into the future.

The Lord be with you.
And also with you.
Lift up your hearts.
We lift them up to the Lord.
Let us give thanks to God.
It is good to give our thanks and praise.

Creator God, maker of earth and sea,
You brought forth life and filled the world with your creation.
You made us from the dust and breathed your Spirit into us that we may live in
your image and care for your world.
When we turned away from you and centered our lives around ourselves,
You sent prophets to warn us and call us back to your way.
In the fullness of time, you sent Jesus to show us how to live.
We join our voices with all creation as we sing in praise to you:

Holy, holy, holy Lord,
God of power and might.
Heaven and earth are full of your glory.
Hosanna in the highest.
Blessed is the one who comes in the name of the Lord.
Hosanna in the highest.

Your holiness is shown to us in Jesus Christ.
In his baptism, your Spirit descended on him.
In the desert, he resisted temptation and followed your call.
In his ministry, he healed the sick and welcomed the outcasts.
In his death and resurrection, he revealed your plan for our lives.

* * *

Remembering your constant faithfulness to us, we take this bread and this cup
And offer ourselves to you to fulfill our promise to live as disciples of Jesus
Christ.

Great is the mystery of faith:

Christ has died.
Christ is risen.
Christ will come again.

Make your Spirit known to us in this bread and this cup
And in the presence of one another
That we may be renewed and strengthened for this Lenten journey together.
Help us to speak of your love and to show it in the ways we care for one
another and for your good earth.
Call us back to faithful lives marked by feeding and caring for the world
around us.
Strengthen us for this journey that we may show your love to all who hunger
for signs of your presence. We ask this in the name of the One who lived as
your presence among us, Jesus the Christ, who taught us to pray. . .

Lord's Prayer

Breaking of the Bread

Come and eat.
As Jesus took bread and gave it to his disciples,
So too we share this bread and cup
That we may encounter the risen Christ among us.
These are God's gifts to share with all who hunger and thirst for new life.

Chapter Five

Praying with the Earth

Our church staff met to make plans for the coming Lenten season. After an opening conversation about our hopes for the congregation during the coming weeks, we decided that it was time for a change in our Lenten observance. We wanted to approach the possibility for spiritual growth in a new way. This year we would focus not on what we might give up during Lent, but on what we longed for in our lives. We chose a biblical theme to explore: "The fruit of the Spirit is love, joy, peace, patience, kindness, generosity, faithfulness, gentleness, and self-control" (Gal. 5:22–23). We hoped to explore what these gifts look like in our lives.

Slowly, a plan began to emerge. At the beginning of the service each week, we would read this text from Galatians and name one of the fruits of the Spirit. We decided to help people in the congregation to visualize the fruits of the Spirit by building a tree in a front corner of the sanctuary. Branches from a beautiful old madrona tree, native to the Pacific Northwest coast, were wired together and placed on a base of rocks and moss. A fountain of water gurgled beneath the tree. We named it the tree of life.[1] In essence, we had crafted a small ecosystem around the tree branches.

Each week as a young member of our congregation read our text from Galatians and we sang a simple song about the gifts of the spirit, another youth in the congregation took a small, framed picture of someone in the congregation and hung it on the tree. The photo was of one of our members whom we identified with the particular fruit of the Spirit we were focusing on that day. Photo frames were shaped like different fruits.

What started as a simple Lenten theme grew into a stunning, beautiful work of art that beckoned us to live into Scripture's call. Week by week, we watched the congregation grow into the vision of this shared life. As we approached Holy Week, Clifton, the custodian, and I got the church's life-sized cross out of the supply closet. We carried the two pieces of the cross on our shoulders, out the basement door, up the hill into the sanctuary, where we assembled them in the other front corner of the sanctuary. Two trees stood before us: the tree of life and the tree of death. Each week the congregation gathered for worship between them in memory and hope.

What we had not recognized when we made these plans was the way using elements of nature would change worship for us. I would like to claim that we had carefully thought all of this through ahead of time or that we had some kind of master plan to create possibilities for theological conversations. In truth, we simply stumbled into a profound way of experiencing and reflecting on ways that faith, life, and the earth converge. The rocks, plants, flowing water, and branches were much more than props. These sights and sounds from nature prompted us to reflect on our experiences in nature: walks in the woods, babbling streams, colors and textures. Suddenly the fruits of the spirit were not only ideals for life in the church; they were woven into our experiences in the world. Joy had a face, and it hung on a tree in our sanctuary.

As we neared Easter, some members of the congregation begged us to leave the tree up front. Not everyone was happy about it, of course. Some complained about the sound of running water during the service. Others complained simply because it was not the way things had always been done in the church. After Easter Sunday, we did take apart both the tree of life and the cross. They were there for a season, and the plants needed sunshine and an opportunity to grow outside. But we promised to create a new tree the next year.

EARTH RHYTHMS

This experience taught me the importance of bringing the earth into our church buildings. It also taught me that engaging with the earth has the power to change the way we see it and ourselves.

Take a moment and consider what natural elements you have experienced in the life of your congregation: a bouquet of cut flowers at the front of the sanctuary each week, or poinsettias at Christmas and lilies at Easter; water in the font (often only when there is a baptism); beeswax candles; some scrappy little palm branches that we hand to our children on Palm Sunday? How can we more fully engage with nature when our experiences with it in church are so limited? When we actually leave our church building to take a walk in the woods, row on a river, or hike up a hillside, we experience the earth in an entirely different way. We delight in its wildness and diversity. We appreciate its beauty as we stroll through gardens. The sounds of nature, from the pounding waves of the surf to the birds chirping in the trees, call out to us. Nature engages all of the senses of our bodies.

Not so long ago humans were much more keenly attuned to the change of the seasons and the earth's reliance on the sun as the source of heat and light. Technological advancements from electricity to air travel, enabling us to fly food across the country, push us farther away from the cycles of nature. While most of us are both dependent on and grateful for modern conveniences, nevertheless the cycle of human life depends on basic elements of sunlight and oxygen.

In our climate-controlled buildings, we easily lose touch with the rhythms of the earth. We flood the long, dark winter days with ambient light. In our worship services, we rarely mention the winter solstice, which marks the return of the light as days grow longer in the Northern Hemisphere. Our vases of cut flowers wilt. When the days of spring arrive and we begin to plant our gardens, we fail to mention our sore knees, aching backs, and dirty fingernails, even in our prayers. Instead, we cling to the "higher, spiritual values" that we have been told to focus on in church.

And yet, the joy that we long for is the joy that we feel when we catch a glimpse of the mountain on our Monday morning drive to work. The hope we yearn for is the hope that flutters in our hearts as a bald eagle unexpectedly soars over our heads. We must find ways to claim and integrate these experiences, so that worship teaches us how to live our days in thanksgiving and praise. In addition, as we examine the way in which our worship services regularly include aspects of creation, we need to ask ourselves the question, what signs are we inviting nature to present to us? Are we making primarily an aesthetic appeal to bring a bit of color to our drab surroundings, or are we ready to engage in more substantive ways with the world around us?

One way to begin the process of bringing nature into our sanctuaries is to reflect on how rhythms and cycles of creation provide ways for us to look at and experience aspects of our faith. In her reflections on baptismal elements (water, oil, and fire), theologian Linda Gibler describes the process of photosynthesis that creates and supports most life on earth. Out of the depth of the oceans, membranes coated with oil emerged and adapted to the sun's light. This dynamic interplay between water, oil, and light released oxygen into the atmosphere, creating the ozone layer that supports diverse life on the planet. Gibler's baptismal prayer includes images of the evolutionary process at work as it supports the emergence of new forms of life on the planet:

> Oil that cradled nascent life in ancient oceans,
> Oil that embraces every cell of every being that ever lived. [2]

Faith acknowledges our dependence on the natural developments of our ecosystem and helps us to see the world as a source of blessing and a place to honor and cherish. Paying attention to the natural rhythms of creation is like listening to the earth's heartbeat. Tracking the solar and lunar cycles of the earth keeps us in touch with forces of gravity that affect our bodies, as the tides ebb and flow and the balance between light and darkness shifts.

Services that reclaim aspects of our dependence on the rhythms of the earth help us to be more aware of these basic elements and to accept our own limits as human beings. For example, celebrating the summer and winter solstice need not be antithetical to Christian faith, but offer an opportunity to reconnect with the gift of light and life that comes from God. While solstice celebrations have been reclaimed by new age and neo-pagan individuals and communities, the church also offers an important perspective when it gives voice to the connections between our dependence on the sun and the earth and our witness to God's action in creating and sustaining the earth. Simple prayers and solstice rituals from an explicitly Christian perspective can draw on the testimony of Scripture as well as theologians and saints of the church throughout its history. Psalms of praise for the gift of light anchor the cele-bration of the summer solstice in the biblical tradition. For example, Psalm 148 offers a good starting place: "Praise him, sun and moon; praise him, all you shining stars! Praise him, you highest heavens, and you waters above the heavens!" (Psalms 148:3–4). St. Francis of Assisi's famous canticle to Broth-er Sun and Sister Moon provides a framework for a liturgy.

> All praise be yours, my Lord,
> In all your creations,
> Especially Sir Brother Sun
> Who brings the day;
> And light you give us through him.[3]

At the time of the winter solstice, the service can focus on another stanza of St. Francis's prayer:

> All praise be yours, my Lord
> For Sister Moon and the Stars;
> In the heavens you have made them,
> Bright and precious and fair.[4]

Accompanying this blessing with the extinguishing of candles to symbolize the longest night of the year before offering a prayer for the return of light provides a way to recognize the changing season.

Services that acknowledge the change of the seasons provide an opportu-nity for pastoral care, particularly to people who are sensitive to the lack of light in the winter. Seasonal Affective Disorder (SAD) strongly affects many who suffer through long winters in the middle and far northern or southern latitudes. Recognizing the rhythms of nature and the earth's cycles as the hours of daylight begin to lengthen provides a way for people to share hope in a communal context. This publicly acknowledges changes that affect us and encourages us to speak more openly with one another about our joys and struggles.

The language of light and darkness often provides a metaphor for struggles in one's spiritual life. The mystic Evelyn Underhill drew on the work of St. John of the Cross and St. Therese to describe the dark night of the soul as a difficult time when doubt nearly overwhelms a person on their faith journey. Attention to the seasonal patterns of light and darkness offers a chance to explore classic spiritual metaphors in light of the earth's rhythms. The earth's transitions from light to darkness are suggestive of different types of spiritual experiences in our own lives and in the congregation. For example, the biblical practice of Sabbath keeping is linked to the earth's need for times of rest and regeneration.

DON'T OBJECT TO OBJECTS

Another good way to open up space for the earth in our worship services is to invite people to bring objects to church that they have found in nature. All religions use objects in their ritual gatherings. The people of ancient Israel carried a tabernacle and elements for worship with them as a way of representing Yahweh's presence accompanying them on their journey. From tea ceremonies to Mayan prayer services, the inclusion of objects, both natural and human made, is a defining feature of religious rituals. For Native Americans, feathers, porcupine quills, animal bones, sage, corn pollen, bark, paints made from plants and minerals, a peace pipe made from stone, and other materials derived from the natural world are basic components of certain rituals. Some rituals use elements directly taken from nature (like feathers) while other ceremonies may transform and adapt natural elements (like the fruit of berries used to paint faces). Zen ceremonies use the process of making and drinking tea to offer spiritual truths to the participants.

Similarly, we see throughout the history of the Christian church a fascination with many objects used in worship, as well as a tension over their presence sometimes when we gather. Even now, museums across the post-Christian European continent are filled with religious objects whose beauty fills the museum cases with a hallowed glow and gives insights into the life of worshipping communities in past centuries. Gold or earthenware communion chalices, pyxides (plural of *pyx*, a container used to hold blessed communion bread), and sprinklers (sometimes called, in the singular, an *aspersorium* or *aspergil*) used in the rite of asperges to sprinkle water (often during a service of baptismal renewal) are but a few of the sacred objects used during Christian worship to facilitate the assembly's liturgy. Throughout its history, the church has utilized all kinds of objects in our worship

services, identified relics for special veneration—and even at times has identified certain places as holy sites for worship and pilgrimage. That is, Christians have recognized the sacredness of particular parts of the earth and
objects (often bones and human remains) that can serve as a focus for Christian devotion.

Even though religions depend on natural and adapted elements for our
rituals, there has also been a history of tension within faith communities
about the use of objects in worship. The Old Testament gives voice to this
struggle. Consider the words of the prophet Amos, who gives voice to Yahweh's rejection of Israel's worship:

> I hate, I despise your festivals,
>   and I take no delight in your solemn assemblies.
> Even though you offer me your burnt-offerings and grain-offerings,
>   I will not accept them;
> and the offerings of well-being of your fatted animals
>   I will not look upon.
> Take away from me the noise of your songs;
>   I will not listen to the melody of your harps.
> But let justice roll down like waters,
>   and righteousness like an ever-flowing stream. (Amos 5:21–24)

Here, the prophetic objection centers on the disconnect between the religious
sacrifices and services, and the faith of the Jewish people as practiced in their
daily lives. Yahweh rejects the pomp and circumstance of the religious gatherings and the people's use of objects because they fail to practice justice and
righteousness in the community.

It is important to note that this critique parallels our observations about
the relationship between ecology and worship in many churches today. Many
people outside of the institutional church point out that Christian worship
(and at times, the daily lives of people within the church) fails to demonstrate
respect and care for creation. As we have already seen, when members of
congregations make connections between their practices of earth care and
their faith, they often act in private, individualistic ways. The task for the
church, then, is to find ways to use objects in worship to enhance our relationship to the earth and build connections to these practices in our daily
lives.

Protestants have had their own unique arguments about using objects in
worship. During the reformation in the sixteenth century, Protestant zealots
damaged many sanctuaries by destroying statues and icons, whitewashing
sanctuaries to cover frescoes, and in other ways purging them of their opu-
lence and emphasis on the material aspects of worship. The display of the
church's power and wealth prompted the destruction of sacred objects in
order to create or reclaim space for worship in keeping with particular inter-

pretations of Scripture. In spite of their emphasis on worship as a primarily spiritual activity, the goal of religious reformers was never to create a space free of objects. (After all, that is not even possible!) Reformers, however, hoped to connect worship practices with daily life by using common elements in services. For example, John Calvin reframed the theology of communion by moving the altar (and its association with sacrifice) away from the front of the sanctuary, where only the priest was allowed to come near to it, and referring to it as a table (a place of nourishment) around which the congregation gathered. This radical redefinition drew on the biblical imagery of table fellowship in the Gospels and the life of the early church, and it pointed to the daily meals that families shared at table in their homes, which Calvin hoped would be a formative time of prayer and fellowship.

Thus, the question is not whether we use objects in worship. It is whether we use them wisely with an eye toward promoting our growth in the life of faith. Encouraging congregations to use objects from nature needs careful and sustained attention. Nature is not designed as a prop for us to employ for our own purposes. Instead, worship planners will want to incorporate elements of nature in ways that provide connections to creation care, the primary goal of their inclusion.

NATURAL ADDITIONS

We can begin imagining new ways of including the earth in our services by paying attention to our own local settings. The rhythm of life in our own neighborhoods provides clues for how to engage in and enrich our experiences. What aspects of nature do we encounter on a regular basis? How can we begin to include these experiences when we gather on Sunday morning?

One way to start including nature more regularly in our worship services is by taking a simple congregational inventory to find out more about the experiences that people have in their gardens, when they visit parks, or when they enjoy other outdoor experiences. What do they enjoy in those settings? How and when are they aware of experiencing God's presence in nature? The goal is to identify a group of shared interests from which worship leaders can draw to prompt reflection about ways we experience the goodness of creation and rely on the earth.

Cultivating a vocabulary that includes local geographical references and our feelings about and relationship to them is an important step. Nature is not simply an amorphous blob outside the sanctuary. This particular river carves its way through our city. These mountains appear on the horizon. This floodplain surrounds us. The simple act of naming the earth around us in our sermons and when we pray begins the slow process of recovering a connection between our faith and this part of the earth on which we live.

Another possibility is to invite people to bring a photo of a special place where they have experienced God's presence. During a prayer for the goodness of the earth, invite people to bring their picture to the front of the sanctuary as an act of thanksgiving for their experience of God's Spirit in the world. This offering of photos can easily be taken one step farther by incorporating them on a bulletin board or as part of a banner to use in worship. Newsletter articles can follow up on this theme. Effective leaders use these activities as a way to begin conversations about how our experience of God in the world connects to the way we express our faith in church.

When designing new ritual elements, the best approach is to create layers of the experience. For example, start by inviting people to bring an object found in nature to a worship service and then to come forward and place it at the front of the sanctuary during the service. This provides a basic way to include creation in our worship space. However, a more integrative approach is to deepen and build on this process, so that these objects can be used to create something as they are brought together.

A group of women in a congregation on the Oregon coast took the seashells that members brought to a service and strung them together as part of a banner that the church hangs in the sanctuary. Fall leaves collected during a prayer of thanksgiving were used for mulch in the church's community garden. For a service of baptismal renewal, participants were asked to bring a small container of water that they collected from nature. Here, the connection became clear that the water of baptism comes from the water sources we rely on every day. As the choir sang the hymn "There Is Water in the Font," participants came forward and filled the font with rainwater, as well as water from nearby rivers and lakes. After a prayer of thanksgiving for the gift of water, the pastor took branches from an evergreen tree, dipped them in the water, and sprinkled water on people as he walked around the sanctuary. In larger sanctuaries, the pastors may take small bowls of water from the font and carry them through the congregation, dipping branches into the bowls and sprinkling water on the congregation. [5]

Including elements from nature in our worship creates connections between our faith and the world around us. We can start as simply as adding a time of blessing for those planting gardens each spring. Invite people to bring an object from their garden to the service. As people enter the church, collect shovels, hoes, gardening gloves, seeds, or other items and place them in one or more wheelbarrows. Youth can wheel the objects to the front of the sanctuary during the offering, and a blessing for a productive season of planting and growing can be offered, so that we will recognize God's sustaining presence as we plant and tend our gardens. Similarly, at the end of a growing season, invite people to bring flowers and produce from their gardens as an expression of thanksgiving for the goodness of the earth that sustains us. Food that is brought can be used in a congregational meal or donated to a local food bank. These services help teach people to recognize how their garden work connects to their faith.

Many Unitarian congregations celebrate a ritual known as a "flower communion." The service was created in 1923 by Norbert Capek, a Czechoslovakian church leader, to bring people together to celebrate the diversity of humanity.[6] Participants are invited to bring one flower to the service (from their own garden or another place) and place it in a large vase as they enter the church. During the service, the bouquet of flowers is brought forward while a brief reading similar to this one by poet Alice Berry is offered:

Children of the earth and sky, we are nurtured, sustained, given warmth and light from above and below.
Supported by earth's strong, firm crust, we build our homes, till the fields, plant our gardens and orchards.
When we turn from self and seek to be aware, we will find holy light in human faces, in blossom, birdsong, and sky.
Then earth is truly our home, and we are
one with all earth's creatures,
Parents of earth's children yet to be.[7]

At the close of the service, participants are invited to select a flower (different from the one that they brought) as an expression of their appreciation for the beauty and diversity of creation. The uniqueness of each single flower provides a metaphor for the unique gifts of each individual, while the beauty of the whole bouquet illuminates the possibility created when we combine our gifts as a community. The poignancy of this ritual grew out of Capek's own biography. He was arrested by the Nazis in Prague because his message of human worth and dignity was deemed as "too dangerous to the Reich [for him] to be allowed to live."[8] He was sent to a concentration camp in Dachau, where he was killed during a medical experiment.

The flower communion service was introduced to congregations in the United States during the 1940s and remains an important way of honoring the earth and respecting the diversity of creation and humanity. While Protestant congregations do not consider this ritual a sacrament, they may choose to adapt elements of the service while continuing to respect the power and simplicity of its historic role among Unitarians.

The sounds we hear in nature also provide a connection to the earth but rarely enter our sanctuaries. Our buildings and sound systems cut us off from the aural experiences in the world around us. Engaging with creation during our worship services can include sounds of nature. At a recent chapel service at my seminary, the call to confession was a recording of birds singing.[9] Songbirds in full praise prompted us to acknowledge the ways that we had cut ourselves off from grace. Following a unison prayer of confession, we raised our voices in praise, joining with the sounds of God's creation. At another chapel service, Scottish sheep sounds (found on YouTube) accompanied our songs from the Iona community. Hearing sounds from nature during our worship helps us to see that Christian faith embraces the world around us. These experiences not only are important for our time in the sanctuary but also help us reframe our daily experiences, when we hear birds tweeting or sheep bleating, by associating these sounds with our worship. Similarly, placing a small water pump in a baptismal font will create movement and the sound of running water. This small step animates stagnant water by adding oxygen to it. By taking these steps, we are creating connections and prompting a dialogue between the sounds of nature and our worship in church.

At a recent retreat I led, I invited participants to take a walk outside during our break and to bring back something from nature that we could use in our worship time. One woman came back with sprouts of wild onion that she collected in a field near our retreat center. As we prayed, we rubbed the green sprigs and smelled the fragrant shoot. During a guided meditation, we reflected on the rhythms of the earth and the way in which the earth provides us with our daily food. Handing out small sprigs of herbs at the beginning of a service engages people's senses as a way of connecting them to the earth.

At Passover celebrations, our Jewish brothers and sisters rely on the powerful symbolism of herbs and other special foods to help them relive the experience of the exodus. The bitter taste of horseradish accompanies the story of the difficult days of slavery in Egypt.

Providing an olfactory accompaniment can enrich the way that we hear Scripture. Creating associations between stories, emotions, and odors can provide a powerful way to open up texts and enrich our lives. Consider handing out cloves of garlic or sprigs of rosemary to the congregation and inviting them to feel and smell them as you read a passage that refers to herbs (e.g., Numbers 11:5[10]). The herbs can be collected at the end of the service and used in preparing a congregational meal. Handing out small pieces of frankincense and myrrh to accompany the reading of the magi's visit to baby Jesus may allow us to experience elements of the birth narrative in Matthew 2. Using perfume or oil to accompany the story of Mary anointing Jesus's feet (John 12) prompts a fuller engagement with the story.

The use of incense in worship to engage the senses remains an important element in many Jewish and Christian services throughout history. The psalmist sees the smoke of the incense as a form of prayer: "Let my prayers be counted before you as incense, and the lifting up of my hands as an evening sacrifice" (Psalms 141:2). Ironically, in spite of the preponderance of biblical support for using incense in worship, many Protestants view incense with suspicion. Here is one more way that some churches have failed to engage our body and senses when we worship God. Reclaiming the use of incense as part of our worship life is another step in the fuller recovery of worship that appeals to our whole bodies.

Creating sensory experiences that accompany prayer and reflection on Scriptural passages makes a map in our memories that associates sounds, smells, and even taste with faith practices. These experiences help us break free of the notion that faith is only an intellectual idea to which we assent. Christian faith, our senses can remind us, is primarily incarnation. It is about our bodies and this planet, all of which are created and sustained by a God whose Spirit dwells with us and among us.

TAKING IT ALL IN

Including nature in our worship services helps us look at the world around us in a more holistic way. In an earlier chapter, we examined the temptation to include elements from creation in our services solely for their aesthetic appeal. If we simply display the most picturesque photos and objects from nature, then we are guilty of commodifying it for our own purposes. Such an approach fails to come to terms with the chaotic aspects of the earth's storms, hurricanes, earthquakes, and other natural disasters.[11] Rather than recognize the diversity and interrelatedness of creation, we rely on an ego-centered perspective that places humans in a privileged position and views the world primarily in terms of its usefulness (e.g., as a nice place). The transition to an eco-centered approach prompts us to look more holistically at nature, to see both the world's beauty and its wildness.

When we welcome the earth more fully into our worship services, we will need to provide room for both thanksgiving and lament. The Old Testament provides ample examples of pleas for the healing of the land. The prophet Jeremiah describes Israel's unfaithfulness as the cause of their experience of a God-forsaken land:

> I looked on the earth, and lo, it was waste and void;
>   and to the heavens, and they had no light.
> I looked on the mountains, and lo, they were quaking,
>   and all the hills moved to and fro.
> I looked, and lo, there was no one at all,
>   and all the birds of the air had fled.
> I looked, and lo, the fruitful land was a desert,
>   and all its cities were laid in ruins
>   before the Lord, before his fierce anger. (Jeremiah 4:23–26)

Jeremiah's vision of the earth's plight recognizes a connection between Israel's faith in Yahweh and the ability of the land to prosper and become fruitful. God's blessing on the earth is integrally tied to human awareness of our responsibility in caring for and maintaining the ecosystem. Flourishing and suffering alike are related to our interactions with the earth, our neighbors, and to God.

Worship should make space for the community to respond in gratitude for the beauty of nature as well as to recognize and pray for the earth's need of healing. One way to show this connection in our congregations is by juxtaposing photos of the scars of the earth during a song of praise. As we see how human actions damage our environment, we are invited to live out our praise of God by working to preserve the beauty of nature. For example, consider singing "For the Beauty of the Earth" while viewing images of the damage caused by fracking,[12] thus holding the earth's lament and suffering alongside a vision of God's blessing. Prayers for the earth's healing and renewal can lead to a commitment to work for justice and sustainable earth care practices.

CONCLUSION

We have examined different ways of including nature in our worship services. Simple practices that include elements from creation will enrich our worship and begin to build bridges connecting our experiences in nature with those in church. As the walls of separation between church and the earth come down, we will discover ourselves planning worship in more holistic ways and interacting with nature from a faith perspective. In this process, we cultivate ways to encourage people to make connections between Christian faith and our daily lives. Along the way, we will discover that our sanctuaries are not places to retreat from the world, but places in which the world can prompt us to worship God.

Liturgical Resources

EASTER SEASON

Christ is risen. Alleluia.
We are the body of Christ.
Each of you is part of the body of Christ.
Alleluia. Christ is risen indeed.

Prayer of Thanksgiving for Creation[13]

Hear these words of Scripture: Rejoice always, pray without ceasing, give thanks in all circumstances; for this is the will of God in Christ Jesus for you. Together, let us give thanks for God's grace in our lives and for the goodness of creation.

Creator God, you made this earth and declared it good.
Show us our place in your creation that we may care for the beauty of the earth, and work for clean air and pure water in our streams and lakes.
Make us resurrection people who bring your renewal to our world.
Breathe your Spirit on us that we may share your healing presence with all people and all creatures.
Raise us up as signs of new life for your coming reign, through Christ we pray. Amen.

In our baptism we are marked as God's beloved sons and daughters. Let us as children of the light bring healing and renewal to the world. May our gratitude for God's grace take root in our lives so that we may blossom into signs of hope, and may the power of resurrection raise us up to work for peace and justice.

Prayer of the Day

Almighty God, whom even death could not contain,
　　we rejoice in the glorious morning of the resurrection of your Son.
We glorify you for the inexplicable gift of new life that by your grace you give us, a gift that is
　　refreshing like dew in the morning grass,
　　nurturing like a mother to her new child,
　　transforming like the waves of the sea upon the shore,
　　redeeming like the blooming of new life in the spring.
Grant us, Lord, the humility and grace to live as your redeemed people,
　　bringing restoration and healing to a broken and wounded creation,

We pray through Jesus Christ, in the power of the Holy Spirit, now and forever. **Amen.**

Prayer for Illumination

Gracious God, all creation tells of your glory. By your Spirit, awaken us so that we may see and hear your presence in the world and in this word that we read today. We ask this in the name of Jesus Christ, our brother and guide. Amen.

Prayer of Dedication

Generous God, we offer you these gifts of money to support the work of the church, that we may be a place for the body of Christ to be present in your world. Strengthen us in all that we do so that the story of your love for this world may be known to all people, through Christ we pray. Amen.

EASTER EUCHARIST

Scripture: Meal images from Luke 24 (Emmaus Road)

Invitation to the Table

Hear these words of Scripture:
Behold, I stand at the door and knock,
If those who hear my voice open the door,
I will come in and eat with them
And they with me.
All who hunger and thirst for righteousness are welcome at this table.

The Lord be with you.
And also with you.
Lift up your hearts.
We lift them up to the Lord.
Let us give thanks to God.
It is good to give our thanks and praise.

God, we give you thanks that
In the beginning, you created heaven and earth,
Making all life in your image,
And you declared that all creation was good.
When we turned away from you and plundered the richness of the earth
You continued to call out to us
Through the beauty of the earth
And through prophets who spoke of your mercy and grace.
In the fullness of time, you sent Jesus who taught us to look for your presence
In the lilies of the field and the sparrows in the trees.
So we join our voices in praising you with birds that sing, rocks that cry out,
and with all creation that calls out to you:

Holy, holy, holy Lord,
God of power and might.
Heaven and earth are full of your glory.
Hosanna in the highest.
Blessed is the one who comes in the name of the Lord.
Hosanna in the highest.

We speak of your holiness and we give thanks for our brother Jesus
who showed us the way to work for peace and justice for our world.
In his life, baptism, teaching, death, and resurrection,
We discover your redeeming presence that continues to bring forth new life.

We share this bread made from the grain that grows up out of the earth
And this wine made from grapes that flourish in the sun
To declare your steadfast love that claims us as your beloved sons and daughters.
We offer you our lives that we may become signs of your grace in our world.

Great is the mystery of faith:
Christ has died.
Christ is risen.
Christ will come again.

Send your Spirit upon us and upon this bread and this cup
That these gifts of creation may show us your presence
in our world, in our neighbors, and in our lives.
Send us out into the world that we may work for the coming of your reign.
Help us feed the hungry,
Welcome the stranger,
Clothe the naked,
Care for the sick,
Visit those imprisoned,
And discover your presence there.
Fill us with hope
So that we may share in the resurrection life that you bring to our world.
Unite us in Christ by the power of your Spirit as we offer our thanksgiving to you
the Creator and Sustainer of all.
Amen.

Lord's Prayer
Breaking of the Bread

When Jesus was at table with his disciples
    He took the bread and blessed it,
    Broke it and gave it to them.
    And their eyes were opened and they recognized him.
The disciples turned to one another and said,
    Were not our hearts burning within us
    When the Scriptures were opened to us?
Brothers and Sisters in Christ:
    Taste and see,
    At this table, God's gifts are offered to all.

Chapter Six

Worship beyond the Walls

When I served as a pastor in Tacoma, Washington, pastors from several of the congregations surrounding Wright Park met each spring to plan a sunrise Easter service in the park. Every time, I lobbied for changing the service from its usual format, and each year I lost the battle. Each year a handful of people from several of the churches gathered at dawn in the chilly, damp air of the Pacific Northwest in a small corner of the large park, where we woefully sang big, traditional Easter hymns while accompanied by a slightly off-key trumpeter. It was less of a witness to the resurrection and more of a testimony to the demise of Christendom. Regardless of the planning conversations and talk of changing the service, in the end we always ended up with a service designed for a sanctuary and a large pipe organ.

When we venture outside of our church buildings for worship, we have to think differently about what we do. How will the space change the way that we gather? How can we incorporate our environment into our worship? In the preceding chapter, we explored how we can bring nature into our worship spaces. In the process, we discovered ways that this process challenges us and creates new connections between worship and our daily lives. This chapter explores the more radical act of taking worship outside the walls of our church buildings and discovering how the context can reshape our services.

Often congregations that hold an outdoor service opt for one of two approaches. (1) Like those who planned the Easter service in the park, we try to reproduce a typical church service in completely different surroundings, only to discover that people feel different about themselves and about worship when they are outdoors. The sights and sounds of nature engage our bodies. We cannot script the world outside of our buildings. There will be distractions both in nature and in the sights and sounds that come from other people, cars, and our surroundings. Or (2) we attempt to plan a service based on our memories of church camps. While we can certainly learn about worship from church camps, we must also notice important distinctions. Generally, camps bring together a group of people for an intense, short period of time, often creating powerful, emotional experiences. In contrast, many congregations plan an occasional outdoor service for a summer break, often in conjunction with a church picnic.

Because of the different nature of these particular services, worship planners need to pay special attention to the setting for worship in order to draw on distinctive features from the surroundings. One of the great opportunities of these services is that those who attend them often come with an openness to—and even an expectation of—new experiences. Careful planning—taking advantage of the opportunity to spontaneously respond to cues and presenting issues from the environment—can bring life to the service.

WELCOMING THE WORLD

While the bright Mexican sun shone down around us, we gathered beneath the shade of a tin-roofed, open-air shelter on the large ranch owned by a member of the congregation. The building we usually used for Sunday worship was occupied that day, so we opted to take our service outdoors. At the front of the space, we placed two small folding tables, one with a loaf of bread and a bottle of wine and the other with a small pitcher of water and a clear bowl. Two dogs wandered among our chairs during worship. The sounds of birds accompanied our singing, and insects buzzed as they circled around us. People were in a jovial, relaxed mood as they took in the beauty of the setting and responded throughout the service.

The theme of the day was water, and I spoke about its prominent place in our lives and in the stories of the Bible. On this warm day, I looked out at the high desert countryside. Where rivers ran through the land and arroyos carved a pathway through the rocks, one could easily see occasional patches of green, the effects of the recent rainy season on the land. I slowly walked over to the table with the pitcher of water and poured it into the bowl, celebrating God's call to us in baptism and our response to God's grace. At the time for communion, I invited worshipers to come forward, to stop by this bowl of water, and to dip their hand in the water as a way to remember their connection to the earth as a child of God. This gesture allowed each of us to renew our baptismal promises to live faithfully as followers of Jesus Christ.

Slowly, people made their way forward. I was not exactly sure how they would respond. The congregation was accustomed to a highly structured service, and this liturgy with an extemporaneous communion prayer and an open invitation to baptismal renewal was pushing in new directions. People responded enthusiastically. Even César, one of the dogs, wandered up to receive a blessing from the local priest. The gifts of water, bread, and wine remind us of the extraordinary goodness of God who created this world and who showers grace and love upon us. At the potluck luncheon following the service, participants spoke about how meaningful it was for them to worship in a new way.

Moving beyond the walls of the sanctuary requires leaders to take risks and create experiences that connect our worship to the settings in which we gather. Rather than being in control of our environments, nature takes center stage and prompts us to respond to its cues. Nature cannot be scripted, and effective leaders need to develop the skill to interact with and respond to events as they happen. When the wind blows our scripts away or rain extinguishes our candles, we need to be able to adapt and speak of God's presence in unexpected ways.

Planning should occur on-site in order to gain a clearer sense of the possibilities. What particular aspects of the setting can be incorporated into the service? Is there water nearby to use in a service of baptismal renewal? Are there rocks or shells that members of the congregation can collect for use during the service? What kind of music fits the mood of the setting? For example, at a recent service in a local park, we looked out on the beauty of the James River as it wound its way through the city, as well as the blight of smokestacks belching steam and other emissions into the air. The opportunity for both lament and praise were readily visible.

When we worship outside, we can easily include time for participants to interact with the environment. When we talk about the earth from inside our church buildings, we must do a mental exercise, remembering experiences that we have out there in the world. When we talk about the earth in natural settings, our bodies are directly connected to the earth. For instance, at a chapel service on the grounds of the seminary, we were invited to walk away from our worship circle to contemplate nature. We took time for nature to engage our senses, asking worshipers: What sounds do you hear? What do you smell? When the group came back together, we briefly shared our experiences. Afterward I found myself looking and listening differently to my surroundings when I walked across campus from my office to the library.

Ethicist Larry Rasmussen notes that the Old Testament shows tension regarding worship in natural settings over against places built by humans. Israel's lineage begins with those who till the soil and are connected to the earth: Adam, Cain, Abel, Abraham, Isaac, and Jacob.[1] Jewish holy days have agricultural roots. For example, Pentecost (Shavuot) was a harvest festival. Worshipers gathered in "agricultural centers like Shechem, Hebron, Bethel, and Beersheba, at altars built by farmers near sacred oak trees, where the ritual celebrations were based on the primary harvests."[2] Sacred sites were also associated with natural settings: Moses climbed to the top of Mount

Sinai to commune with God (Exodus 19). Other appearances of God oc-
curred in oak groves or by springs of fresh water.

As priests began to exert their influence, however, worship shifted away
from the natural world. The old altars built of arable topsoil and dedicated to
Yahweh were replaced by elaborate structures built of wood and bronze.
Rasmussen explains the significance of this shift:

> The Yahwist's altar symbolizes the dependence of the people on the land God
> has given them, the land that roots them. The Priestly altar symbolizes the
> achievement of the people who rule the land as mediated by priests. Humility,
> service, and limit contrast with stewardly power and control, with both under-
> stood as commands of God.[3]

While we cannot change these historical developments, we can reclaim aspects of the Israelites' early relationship to the land that sustained our faith
ancestors. As we experiment with worship in nature, we have the opportunity
to reconnect with natural elements that inspired people of faith to recognize
God's presence. Worshipping outside is not an end in itself. The goal is much
larger: to help us integrate our daily lives and experiences through which we
can recognize the divine mystery that is part of all creation.

Native American Christians spoke to me in Tacoma, Washington, about
ways nature prompts them to see the sacred around them. For example, the
cloud at the top of the mountain is a sign of God's mystery, and the trees
point to the divine. (This sacredness prompts our care for trees, or as one
person reported being taught, not to break tree branches, as a way to respect
Mother Earth.) As one member of the Native American congregation told
me, "In the old days, church was anywhere where the Great Spirit was."

LESSONS FROM PENTECOST

Holding services outside of our sanctuaries and paying careful attention to
our setting as we worship in nature provides us an opportunity to draw on
features of the land that inspire us. Gathering in a garden for a harvest
festival offers a chance for us to reclaim aspects of a holy day that we
otherwise fail to notice. When we examine the story of the first Pentecost, we
discover layers in our tradition that will help us reconnect faith to the
rhythms of the earth.

Christians celebrate Pentecost as the birthday of the church. The origin of
this development is recorded in Acts 2, where we read that the disciples and
other followers of Jesus are huddled in Jerusalem. There Jews from around
the ancient world gather for the harvest festival of Shavuot, which occurs
fifty days after the celebration of Passover. (The name Pentecost comes from
the Greek *pente,* or *fifty*.) In ancient Israel, the harvest of grain lasted for fifty

days and ended with the festival of Shavuot, when the first fruits of the harvest were brought to the temple and presented as an offering. Hebrew Scripture provides accounts of the development of this holiday. For example, Exodus 34:22 and Deuteronomy 16:10 describe the proper observance of the festival. Faithful Jews also associate the occasion with the time when God gave the Torah to Israel at Mount Sinai.[4] The gift of the Torah is pictured, like the harvest of the land, as that which gives life and sustains the people.

When Christians gather to celebrate the coming of the Spirit and the birth of the church, we also have the opportunity to connect these events to the cycles and well-being of the land. Exploring the history of Pentecost is a way of opening up a window on the relationship between our religious festivals and their deep connection to the earth. Even though we may live in parts of the world where the harvest cycles are different from those of ancient Israel, when we learn the story of their development, we discover ways that our faith is connected to the health of the earth.

Gathering in a garden or on a farm for a Pentecost service offers us the chance to focus on ways that the birth of the church connects to the earth's needs. When we remain in our pews, we are tempted to think of the church in terms of buildings and institutions. However, when we move our celebration outside, we can more readily see the church as the people who gather to give thanks for God's blessing and goodness.

As we pray for the Spirit to inspire us to care for one another and for the earth, the call to act in ways that support our neighbors and respect the needs of creation become clear. Pentecost is not simply a story about a few people receiving the gift of the Spirit long ago. When we pray for the Spirit, we are not expressing our yearning for self-improvement. Acts 2 is a text that invites us to see church renewal as integrally tied to the plight of the earth. Celebrated as a harvest festival or as a time when plants and fields are beginning to grow, this festival invites us to find our place in the larger ecosystem.

HEARING SCRIPTURE ANEW

Simply reading the Bible in new places can make a powerful difference in how we understand it. When we gather outside, we discover how often Scripture refers to the land. Even familiar texts like Jesus's parables, with their images of the earth and animals, take on new life as we read them in nature. When we read Matthew 6 while birds fly around us and call out to one another, we will hear this text differently: "Look at the birds of the air; they neither sow nor reap nor gather into barns, and yet your heavenly Father feeds them" (Matthew 6:26). When we listen to Jesus's words inviting us to place our trust in God while we sit in a garden surrounded by blossoming flowers, we will respond differently to Jesus's words: "Consider the lilies of the field, how they grow; they neither toil nor spin, yet I tell you, even Solomon in all his glory was not clothed like one of these" (Matthew 6:28–29). Nature can help us interpret and live into these texts: "But strive first for the kingdom of God and his righteousness, and all these things will be given to you as well" (Matthew 6:33).

Seeking to live in light of God's gift of grace prompts us to set aside our own preoccupation with ourselves, our endless concern to place ourselves first, our anxieties over our future, and our futile attempts to control our fate. Instead, hearing Scripture in harmony with the sounds and beauty of the earth invites us to trust in God's goodness to provide for our needs.

Leaders responsible for planning outdoor worship services need to cultivate the skill of reading Scripture from the perspective of the earth. Worship planners should start by looking for references to nature to help them to craft a service that connects us to the environment.

PRAYING WITH THE EARTH

An integral part of worship is to create memories for both our minds and our bodies, and worshipping outside allows us to engage fully in this process. Many people have discovered the spiritual practice of *lectio divina*, an ancient way of listening to Scripture. In this practice, a text is read multiple times, so that participants can listen for words that speak particularly to them. Recently, some worship leaders have proposed adapting this practice to our experiences in the world in what is called *natura divina*.[5] Participants are invited to take time by themselves to observe the world around them. As they walk around, they look for what in this setting communicates the presence of the divine to them. They ask themselves, since the earth is God's creation, how does it call us to deepen our relationships? How does it prompt us to care for ourselves and the earth? In this practice, the earth itself becomes an inspired text for contemplation. As we meditate on particular features, we seek to hear God speaking to us. Afterward, participants can be invited to share their insights with one another. Our learning from our contemplation of creation grows as we hear from one another how each of us sees God's presence in the world.

Congregational leaders can also encourage individuals to deepen their connections between their spiritual practices and the earth. Consider adapting brief services of morning and evening prayer for members of your congregation to use as they take walks or work in their yards and gardens. Several years ago, I decided to make a recording of morning and evening prayer for members of our congregation.[6] The choir and I gathered in the sanctuary to record services of morning and evening prayer from the Book of Common Worship. The services follow the shape of daily prayer that is included in most denominational worship books: a psalm, reading from Scripture, prayers of thanksgiving and supplication, and a familiar song or two. Soon after copies of the recording were distributed to members of the congregation, I started hearing reports about people's experiences with them. People listened on their way to work and spoke of how they helped them approach their day differently. A unique aspect was featuring the voices and sounds of our own community. As the choir sang "Send Forth Your Spirit, O Lord," the percussive sound of the church's ancient furnace banged away in the background.

Adapting the prayers with special attention to our own geographic location encourages people to pray with and for the earth. Philip Newell's wonderful book *Celtic Benedictions* offers a general model for daily prayer in the tradition of Celtic spirituality that draws on elements of the earth to heighten our awareness of God's presence.[7] Language in the prayers names the forces of nature in order to describe our experiences of God. For example, the wild wind whistling through the trees represents the Spirit stirring up our lives. We can adapt this approach by including specific, local features in these prayers for our own congregations. Invite listeners to pray for the health of a local river or to thank God for the presence and beauty of the particular mountains that surround them. Those who are more adventurous might consider making brief videos of morning and evening prayer in nature. Posting them on YouTube provides access not only to members of your own congregation but to members of the broader community.

One way to build on this practice is to invite participants to use these recordings for a specific period of time, perhaps as a Lenten discipline. At the end of this period, invite people to gather for a meal and to relate their experiences to one another. This is a subtle way of encouraging all of us to share our faith by giving testimony of places and ways that we see God at work in our lives. In addition, you will learn ways to improve the process for your next set of recordings. Ambitious leaders may want to develop recordings that highlight seasonal changes in your own region as a way to extend our relationship to the earth throughout the seasons of the year.

Another way to build on the connections between personal prayer and the earth is to write prayers for particular situations. Create a collection of prayers for gardeners as they dig, plant, and tend the earth, or prayers for recreational activities, such as boating or swimming in lakes. Laminating the pages of prayers will allow individuals to use them in their outdoor activities. Our primary goal is to foster a sense of prayer as we go about our daily activities. Prayer sheets provide a tangible resource to encourage individuals to cultivate the practice of praying as they work and play.

HIGHLIGHTING SEASONAL CHANGES

In addition to supporting our spiritual growth in our daily activities, congregational leaders can provide opportunities for people to connect their faith to particular aspects of the earth's rhythm. Many traditions follow lunar cycles when establishing significant holidays. Jews celebrate Passover on the first full moon after the spring equinox. Christians in the West adapted this practice by celebrating Easter on the first Sunday after the first full moon that occurs on or after the spring equinox. [8]

Recognizing the rhythms of the earth's rotation and the significant effect of the moon and sun on planet earth is central in many religious traditions. People in northern Europe gathered for rituals amid standing stones that aligned with the summer and winter solstice. Incan spiritual leaders built Machu Picchu with its stunning chapels that allowed them to track the sun, moon, and stars. These early astronomers perceived an intricate correlation between the universe and spirituality. Visiting these sites today still prompts wonder and awe at the mysterious ways in which these incredible edifices were built, as well as curiosity about what went on when people gathered for their celebrations.

What aspects of creation and seasonal changes can you pay attention to in your area? On a pleasant, winter evening, a member from the congregation in central Mexico where I occasionally preach led my wife and me to a botanical garden. We hiked up to the top of a hill that overlooks San Miguel de Allende, a town with a population of about 150,000 located in the high desert country northwest of Mexico City. We were joined by others coming to celebrate the full-moon ceremony. Inside the gates, we listened to the beat of drums urging us forward and calling us to gather. As we walked down the path, we caught our first glimpse of a large, glowing, orange-colored moon appearing on the horizon. We met in a large opening, formed a circle, and passed around rhythm instruments to use during the ceremony. As the moon rose in the sky, we sang a chant together, giving thanks for the goodness of life and the gifts of Mother Earth. We turned to face the moon and stared in wonder as it beamed down upon us. One by one people called out prayers of thanksgiving and petitions. We prayed for the healing of the earth and for the end of violence. We gave thanks for the food that comes from the earth and the presence of family and friends. We raised our arms in openness toward the sky to receive the blessings that the sky rains down upon us. Here, in touch with the earth beneath our feet, surrounded by the beauty of trees, cacti, and other desert plants, we breathed deeply of the cool, evening air that revives us at the end of the day.

When we adapt rituals that are based on the cycles of nature by adding distinctive Christian themes, we should be attentive to the risks of syncretism and triumphalism. *Syncretism* is claiming that all religious systems hold the same set of goals and values. *Triumphalism* means simply Christianizing the rituals and belief systems of other traditions by inserting our own language and perspectives. Instead, our goal should be to recognize that all religious rites and traditions use the basic stuff of the earth to express beliefs that we share as well as those that we articulate in unique ways. As Christians, our belief in the Trinity provides a distinctive perspective on how to respectfully appropriate earth rituals within a Christian framework. Recalling God as creator, Christ as Immanuel/God with us, and the Spirit as the life-giving presence among us provides a theological foundation for articulating how the universe is interrelated. When we sing the words of Joseph Renville's hymn, we have an opportunity to name how the cycles of the earth, sun, and moon sustain our lives:

> Many and great, O God, are thy things,
> Maker of earth and sky.
> Your hands have set the heavens with stars;
> your fingers spread the
> mountains and plains.
> Lo, at your word the waters were formed;
> deep seas obey your voice.
> Grant unto us communion with you, O star-abiding One.
> Come unto us and dwell with us;
> with you are found the gifts of life.
> Bless us with life that has no end,
> eternal life with you.[9]

In our praise for the gift and intricacies of the solar system, we acknowledge God's handiwork in the mysteries of the universe. Because of the Christian commitment to the doctrine of the incarnation, we see Christ's continued presence among us as a sign of God's grace on earth. The Spirit that animates us moves in our midst and continues to renew us. Thus, a service of thanksgiving for the natural order of the universe, including solar and lunar cycles, serves as a Christian act of praise in the name of the Trinitarian God whom we know and worship.

From this perspective, the closer we become attuned to the cycles of nature, the more clearly we see God's presence in the world around us. Paying attention to the earth's cycles is a way of noticing our place in the universe and the rhythms of the earth, our home. Or, to quote the famous words of essayist Wendell Berry: "The care of the Earth is our most ancient and most worthy and after all our most pleasing responsibility. To cherish what remains of it and to foster its renewal is our only hope."[10] Our cherishing of the earth grows out of our deepening awareness of the earth's inner workings and our gratitude for the way the earth provides for our needs. In this act of recognition, as Christians we see God's presence in all the rhythms of the universe.

GOING FULL CIRCLE

Groups from diverse backgrounds integrate earth-centered rituals and practices into our worship in different ways. Congregational leaders will need patience and creativity when developing outdoor worship services, earth prayers, or other rituals that draw on our relationship to and dependence on the earth. Some congregational members will welcome these services, while others will resist them and may even describe the services as pagan. As we saw in chapter 1, the church has a long tradition of promulgating a theology that primarily describes the earth in utilitarian terms. Accompanying new practices with educational opportunities, chances for feedback, and frequent explanations in church newsletters and other congregational publications will help inform congregational members and calm the fears of those who will worry about new approaches and practices. (You can still expect to hear, "We have never done this before!")

The road to recovering an eco-centered theology will be slow and challenging at times. Effective leaders listen for opportunities to present new ideas and practices at a sustainable pace and in ways that help shape congregational identity and create openness to responding to God's presence throughout creation.

Some congregations already bring an openness to exploring intersections between Christian faith and other traditions' ways of respecting the sacredness of the earth. On a recent trip to Guatemala, a small group of teachers and students from my seminary met with Daniel Caño on a Sunday afternoon in an Episcopal Church in Quetzaltenango. Daniel is an active member of the congregation who studied theology at the Evangelical Center for Pastoral Studies in Central America (CEDEPCA) in Guatemala City. As a person of Mayan ancestry, Daniel also draws on his indigenous heritage to sustain his spirituality. He spoke to our group about how many Mayan Christians see connections between Christian faith and the ways of their ancestors.

Daniel explained that like many other indigenous traditions, Mayan spirituality draws on the earth as a primary source for its rituals. He then described to us the ancient Mayan fire ceremony, which recognizes the basic elements of earth, air, water, and fire. In the prayer, these elements are associated with the four directions: (1) The east, the direction of the rising sun, is symbolized by fire and the color red. (2) The west, the direction of the setting sun and darkness, is symbolized by earth and the color black. (3) The south as the source of water, which brings seeds to life, is symbolized by the color yellow. (4) The north is symbolized by air and the color white. The colors of green and blue at the center of the Mayan cross represent natural and spiritual energy. This ceremony helps participants by guiding them to reflect on sources and elements that support life on earth.

Some Christian communities in Guatemala welcome Mayan ceremonies, viewing them as complementary to Christian faith. Our group met in Antigua with Father Atilio Prandina, who incorporated aspects of the ceremony as part of the Roman Catholic services that he led during his ministry in Mayan communities in the mountains of Guatemala. In adapting rituals from other cultures, participants should show respect for other traditions, as well as discern how these traditions can support Christian practices that draw from the earth and encourage creation care.

When we returned to the United States, our group led a chapel service at our seminary that adapted parts of the Mayan ceremony for the prayers of the people.

Participants face east, where a red candle is lit:
We pray for the presence of God at the time of beginnings.
Lord, hear our prayers.
Participants face west, where a black candle is lit:
We pray for the presence of God at the time of endings.
Lord, hear our prayers.
Participants face north, where a white candle is lit:
We pray for the presence of God as felt through the life-giving wind.
Lord, hear our prayers.
Participants face south, where a yellow candle is lit:
We pray for the presence of God in the seeds that will one day grow into the plants, animals, and people of this world.
Lord, hear our prayers.
Participants turn toward the center of the room, where green and blue candles are lit:
We pray for the presence of God in the struggle to see the unity of the spiritual and physical world in which we live.
Lord, hear our prayers. [11]

A primary goal of this prayer is to incorporate aspects of Mayan spirituality that we learned about during our visit to Guatemala in a way that broadens our practices and orients our faith to the natural elements of the earth that are shared by all cultures and traditions.

CONCLUSION

In this chapter, we have explored a wide array of approaches to creating services beyond the walls of our sanctuaries. From simply praying in nature to adapting earth-centered practices from other traditions, eco-centered churches make opportunities to explore new paths that will enrich our spirituality and more closely align us with life on earth. As we branch out, we will discover new ways of reading Scripture and new possibilities for reclaiming our theological heritage of honoring and respecting the earth, and seeing it as a witness to God's presence.

Liturgical Resources

PENTECOST

Let us speak of God.
Let us sing with creation.
May God's Spirit fill us with awe and wonder.
May the Spirit bring us the gift of understanding.
All: **Together we may see the world as God's good gift.**

Prayer of the Day

God our Creator, maker of earth and sea and sky,
We give you honor and glory for your good works of creation,
    and we thank you for the grace that sustains us.
Teach us to feel in the winds that refresh us the wind of the Spirit,
    to see in the fiery sun your consuming flame of cleansing and renewal,
    to taste in bread and wine the fertile goodness of your earth,
    to hear in rolling waters all of creation's cry for justice.
Let your Spirit of holiness blow through us, shine on us, fill us, wash over us
with your passion for all of creation, all creatures and living things,
Through your Son, Jesus Christ our Lord,
    who lives and reigns with you and the Spirit,
    Three in One, One in Three, now and forever.
Amen.

Confession and Pardon

"The promise is for you, for your children, and for all who are far away, everyone whom the Lord our God calls." Let us hear and respond to God's call to us today. Let us repent and live into the good news together:

God of all creation, we confess that we have divided your world and used it for our own good rather than for the common good. We have plundered the earth rather than caring for it. Forgive us for turning away from you and your creation and for failing to understand one another. Unite us with a vision of wholeness and the outpouring of your Spirit that we may live together in unity and peace. Amen.

Assurance of Pardon

Hear these words of Scripture: "God has made known to us the ways of life;
Make us full of gladness with God's presence."

Brothers and sisters, in Jesus Christ our sins are forgiven.
Let us live as forgiven people by caring for all who are in need and for all creation.

Prayer for Illumination

Spirit, breathe on your word and on us, that as we hear your word, we may welcome and devote ourselves to it. Unite us as a community that cares for one another as a sign of your kingdom, through Christ we pray. Amen.

Prayer of Dedication

Giving God, we offer ourselves and what you have provided for us in order that we may care for those in need. Bless us with your Spirit that we may praise God with glad and generous hearts. Amen.

PENTECOST EUCHARIST

Scripture: Meal images from Acts 2

The rushing wind calls out your name.
The light dances in praise to you.
The Spirit comes as we gather here to pray and break bread.
Come, all who long to share this way of life together.

The Lord be with you.
And also with you.
Lift up your hearts.
We lift them up to the Lord.
Let us give thanks to God.
It is good to give our thanks and praise.

God of earth, air, wind, and fire,
You created life and set us in the world to live in harmony and justice.
When we turned away from you and ignored the signs of your presence,
you sent prophets, dreamers, and visionaries to show us your way.
In the fullness of time, Jesus of Nazareth performed deeds of power, wonders,
and signs to point us to you.
So we join in song with them and with all creation as it praises you:

Holy, holy, holy Lord,
God of power and might.
Heaven and earth are full of your glory.
Hosanna in the highest.
Blessed is the one who comes in the name of the Lord.
Hosanna in the highest.

Holy are you, O God.
We give thanks for Jesus who taught us of your way.
In his life, death, and resurrection,
he gave witness to your faithful presence.
And promised us that you would send us your Spirit
that we may see and hear again the message of salvation
that you weave through all of creation.

* * *

Remembering how your Spirit brings us new life,
We take this bread and cup to celebrate your presence among us.
We offer ourselves to join in the Spirit's work of bringing healing and hope
to this world that you created and that you love.

Great is the mystery of faith:
Christ has died.
Christ is risen.
Christ will come again.

Pour out your Spirit on all who gather here
And on these gifts of bread and cup
That in sharing this meal together
We may encounter the risen Christ among us.
Give us wonders and signs of your presence in all the earth.
Strengthen us through your word, through fellowship,
Through breaking bread together, and through our prayers,
which we offer in Christ's name. Amen.

Lord's Prayer
Breaking of the Bread

Day by day,
They spent much time together
In worship and in breaking bread
And they ate their food with glad and generous hearts
Praising God and having the goodwill of all people.

Chapter Seven

The Earth as Home

As a young boy, I sat on a wooden pew and sang the words of the old Gospel hymn:

> This world is not my home I'm just a passing through
> My treasures are laid up somewhere beyond the blue
> The angels beckon me from heaven's open door
> And I can't feel at home in this world anymore. [1]

Perhaps the words were meant primarily as an expression of longing for union with a God who was viewed as "up in heaven." Nevertheless, this theology shaped the way our congregation thought about the earth. We overlooked our wooden pews and brick walls, even as we took those materials from the earth's resources. At best, we viewed it in utilitarian terms, something to use for materials until we reached our final destination. We might notice the earth's beauty from time to time, but our attachment to it was temporal. At worst, we approached the earth as disposable. Any reason to care for creation was ultimately trumped by the conviction that the earth's value was limited to the resources we could take from it. Within this theological system, we looked at ourselves in similar ways. We viewed our bodies as coats wrapped around eternal souls, which some day would be released from the bondage of this earth.

When I reflect on the sources of this theology, I am shocked by how much of the Bible was simply ignored. From the opening confession in Genesis that God created the heavens and the earth and declared them good, to the closing vision in Revelation of God redeeming this earth by making all things new, Scripture testifies to the many ways that people of faith have discovered God by contemplating this world, rather than simply hoping to escape it. Thus, the starting place for Christians who are committed to caring for creation as an integral part of our faith is to reread and engage with Scripture as a primary resource. We will be required to critique many of the assumptions and theologies that we often bring to texts. We can picture this process as a form of weeding out the misinterpretations from our biblical garden. Much like invasive weeds that take over our yards and choke out the flowers we planted, the roots of theological systems that interfere with the sensitive interconnections of this ecosystem will have to be dug up and pulled out.

As we have seen, some interpretations of the creation stories in Genesis are viewed as license to plunder the earth or a rationale to use natural resources to support human progress, without considering the well-being of all forms of life on the planet, must be removed. The King James translation of Genesis 1:26–27 uses the word "dominion," which reinforced this theological interpretation. Some argue that this text provides a divine authorization for humans to conquer the earth. In the act of digging out these destructive elements, we will discover layers of our theology that are still infected by this approach. Even the milder language of claiming that humans were appointed stewards of creation often reinforces the idea that humanity has a higher place in the system. As Christians, we will continue to struggle with finding our right place within this ecosystem until we fully embrace a theology that respects the earth as God's gift and accept our role as humans by cherishing the earth and caring for it.

The corrective task of rereading and reappropriating Scripture can help us discover a modest, but crucial role for humans to play within the ecosystem. We have noted a variety of ways of hearing Scripture in different settings inside and outside our church buildings, as well as learning to pray with and for creation, all of which will help reorient our theology toward the needs of the earth. As we go about the hard work of reclaiming Scripture as a primary source for addressing the environmental crises that face us, we will discover how our actions of caring for the earth are an integral part of our faith commitment. With this focus, the church is helping people discover and articulate connections between our Christian commitment and our response to the needs of the earth. No longer will we expect individuals to make associations on their own. Instead, the church will establish its role in nurturing a spirituality that seeks the well-being of all creation.

This transformative work requires us to reorient our priorities and develop new resources. It is not enough to simply have a service on Earth Day. Incremental change will not address the needs of the planet in this time of ecological crisis, nor will it bring about the renewal that the church desperately needs. Instead, the church needs to radically reexamine its primary liturgical commitment to Word and Sacrament in an effort to connect us with our care for creation. The church can respond to our contemporary context by revising its resources and calling Christians to make a contribution to the work of caring for the earth. Ethicist Dieter Hessel observes, "Theologians of the church need to give explicit attention to the environmental aspects of biblical narratives, ethical teachings, confessions of faith, the sacraments of baptism and holy communion, and hymns and prayers. With this new sensibility, Christian worship resources need to be reassessed and revised."[2]

There is widespread agreement among scientists about the severity of the current ecological crisis and its effect on climate change, as well as the importance of promoting ecological diversity and sustainability. Theologian Thomas Berry refers to the task of global eco-justice as "the Great Work" of our time.[3] This work, according to Lutheran pastor Paul Santmire, requires "a plethora of global communities and constituencies" to take up the task of "envisioning and the establishing of a truly just and beautifully viable earth community."[4] In this global context, it is incumbent upon faith communities to contribute our voices to the effort to care for the earth and respond to the ecological demands of our time. Santmire concludes, "Christians today must be radically realistic, radically committed to telling the whole truth, because nothing less than the future of the world God sent Jesus Christ to save—more specifically, the future of life as we know it on Planet Earth—is at stake."[5] Similarly, Larry Rasmussen calls for Christian communities to adapt their teachings and practices in order to address the ecological crisis that we are facing and to offer a constructive theology that responds to issues in nature and culture "so as to prevent their destruction and contribute to their sustainability."[6]

While ecclesial bodies and theologians continue to stress the importance of the church's response to the ecological crisis, Santmire underscores the need for the church's liturgy to reflect this pressing priority. He claims that a primary task is "to encourage and to help the ecumenical churches, especially those that take the liturgy as a historic given, to renew their worship, precisely in order to make possible more meaningful, more effective, and more passionate Christian participation in the quest to accomplish the Great Work of our time."[7]

As we reclaim the role of Scripture and its focus on the earth, we note the need to regularly bring elements of the earth into our worship. Our prayers and even the stuff that we use in worship shape our responses to the earth. When we seal ourselves inside our sanctuaries and away from the world, we unwittingly reinforce the sense that the church is removed from the needs of the world. In order to immerse ourselves in a theology of earth care, we must engage all our senses in worship as we support care for the environment. Praise for the beauty of creation, lament for the earth's plight, confession for our misuse of the earth's resources, testimonies of our actions rooted in our faith language, prayers that name the blessings and needs of our local environment—all serve to prompt us to worship in a way that expresses and embodies an eco-centered Christian faith. The demands of our time require

that the church reread Scripture and expand our vision of the sacraments to
deepen our commitment to honoring our relationship to the earth.

FOLLOWING THE SACRAMENTS INTO THE WORLD

On this journey to a faith that is more closely connected to creation, the
church brings its theology and practice of baptism and Eucharist. In the
sacraments, the church takes stuff from the earth and uses it to celebrate
God's presence among us. The first followers of Jesus gathered over meals to
share stories from his life and ministry. In sharing these memories, they
experienced the presence of the risen Christ among them. Wine, water, bread,
and other food were shared with those who responded to Jesus's call to
discipleship. The earth itself provided the resources for the church's celebration. The act of belonging to this community was marked by pouring water
over newcomers or immersing their bodies into rivers or lakes. Nature itself
provided the venues for the church to celebrate its growth as a community.

While baptism and communion are distinctive Christian acts, they point
beyond the gestures themselves by inviting us to broaden our engagement
with and in the world. Rather than seeing the sacraments as special actions
for a privileged few who huddle inside the walls of our sanctuaries, in baptism and communion we use elements of the earth to make claims about the
presence of God's grace in the world around us. Celebrating the sacraments,
then, carries with it the power to push us into the world rather than remove us
from it. Just as the church must reclaim the witness of Scripture to attune us
to the needs of the earth, so we need to reclaim the sacraments themselves as
acts that link us to the earth.

This bread that we break and eat together and this wine that we pour and
share are gifts from the resources of the earth. The wheat and grapes rely on
the nutrients from the earth's soil, from the rainwater that nourishes, from the
sun that shines brightly down and helps them to grow. When we gather
around a table to speak of God's redemptive presence in our lives, we tell this
story with the earth's resources. The first Christians found that sharing a
meal around these stories of God's grace taught them how to live as a community that shared its resources and cared for one another. The Eucharist as
shared meal became a sacrament that celebrated the goodness of the world
that God creates, sustains, and redeems even as it orients participants to the
place of humans in this cosmic story. As they ate and drank together, they
debated interpretations of texts and stories. In the process, they discovered
shared values that supported their commitment to follow Jesus Christ.

Similarly, this water that we use in baptism comes from the earth. It is not
any more sacred or less sacred than the other water on which we rely for life.
The church relies on the gift of water as a way to celebrate God's call and

claim on our lives. When we gather around fonts or enter baptismal pools to celebrate God's love for us as beloved sons and daughters, we use water to mark ourselves as followers of Jesus Christ. In this act, the water of baptism connects us with the testimonies of others who throughout the church's history have responded to God's call. Looking at the water around us with eyes of faith prompts us to care for the earth. The rivers that run through our cities, the ponds and lakes that we camp by each summer, the water that we pipe into our homes for drinking, bathing, and cleaning—all point to the presence of the divine in our lives. The One who calls us and claims us also provides for our basic needs. Each time we turn on the faucet, take a shower, or sip a cool glass of water, we encounter an opportunity for thanksgiving. Christians see water as that which unites us in this family of faith. The effort to provide clean, safe water for all people is an act of compassion and evangelism. We trust that the goodness of creation points to God, who is the source of life.

LIFE IN CHRIST

With the sacraments as a guide for how to include our bodies in worship, we can examine other options that more fully engage our senses and connect us to the world around us. By paying attention to features of our local geographic area, we can engage in worship practices that connect us to the land on which we live. By displaying photos of places that we drive by each day or using collections of rocks or plants from our area, worship helps us to look at the earth around us as God's good creation. When we hear Scripture's vision for the healing of the nations while viewing photos of people working to clean up a local river, we are creating associations between how we read the Bible and how we work for justice. When we pray for local farmers during planting season while we hold seeds or grain in our hands, we remind ourselves of our dependence on God, the earth, and those who grow our food. When we come to the communion table with bags of groceries to give to the local food bank, we are engaging in bodily practices of thanksgiving and demonstrating care for our neighbor.

Worship that engages our senses with elements from creation trains us to connect Word and Sacrament to the needs of the earth. Both inside our sanctuaries and in services outdoors, we learn to look at the world around us and respond in light of our faith. When our faith connects us to the earth, we take our place in the long line of faithful people who have seen the earth as a theater of God's glory. The great German theologian Dietrich Bonhoeffer once observed that the church provides physical space for the body of Christ in the world.[8] From this perspective, the church building itself serves as a sign of God's presence on earth.

In these spaces, Christians gather not to separate ourselves from the earth, but to claim the earth as a place where the body of Christ is present. As the baptized, beloved children of God, we are incarnational signs of God's commitment to redeem creation. When we gather for worship, we do so not to take refuge from the world, but to bear witness to the ongoing presence of the resurrected Christ. A theology of incarnation celebrates all the places where we encounter God.

Scripture pictures the earth as that which God speaks into existence. All of life draws on God as its source. God shapes humans from the dust of the earth and breathes life into us, so that we may live in God's image. An incarnational theology, then, looks at the earth and at human life as places and occasions to encounter the divine. Christians confess that Jesus Christ is Immanuel, God with us, and that when we celebrate the sacraments, we are united in Christ.

On this image, the apostle Paul built a portrait of the church as those who are "in Christ." New Testament scholar Michael Parsons surveys the diverse ways that Paul uses this language and concludes that it functions as both a theological claim and an ethical exhortation. To be "in Christ" combines both personal and corporate components: "Therefore we have been buried with him by baptism into death, so that, just as Christ was raised from the dead by the glory of the Father, so we too might walk in newness of life" (Romans 6:4). This new life in Christ combines our personal response to Jesus's call to follow him with the community that welcomes and nurtures us in a life of faith. Paul recognizes that in baptism we participate in a communal ritual in which our immersion in water reenacts the death and resurrection of Jesus Christ. In this ritual, we are absorbed into a community of believers who confess faith in Christ as the one who makes God known to us.

There is, though, another layer to this language. Parsons points to the "cosmic significance" of this expression.[9] Baptism unites us with the Gospel story of Christ's death and resurrection and the church's profession of faith in the cosmic Christ. In his letter to the church in Colossae, Paul presents Christ as God's incarnation, which holds the cosmos together:

> He is the image of the invisible God, the firstborn of all creation; for in him all things in heaven and on earth were created, things visible and invisible, whether thrones or dominions or rulers or powers—all things have been created through him and for him. He himself is before all things, and in him all things hold together. (Colossians 1:15–17)

Paul pulls together the threads of incarnation and creation, weaving a theological tapestry that portrays the place of humans in the universe. We exist within this vast system, which ultimately finds its coherence in God. For Christians, the incarnation of Christ gives particular shape to the divine body that stretches out across the universe. To be "in Christ" is to live and breathe as part of this carefully designed and interrelated system. Our assent to God's call is an assent to care for one another and for the earth. This vision of the church and Christian life invites us to participate in God's redemptive work of bringing healing and renewal to the earth.

COMMUNAL SUPPORT

When we gather for worship, we come as followers of Jesus Christ. Worship as an act of the community underscores that Christian faith is neither private nor individualistic. We share certain practices as we gather around word, water, bread and wine. Understanding Scripture is a communal act guided by the Spirit's presence among us. The sacraments of baptism and communion are actions of the assembly that gathers to worship. These corporate practices shape and nurture faith. Together, we respond to God's call to work for the coming of God's reign. Together, we work for justice for people who are oppressed, as well as for the healing of the earth and the well-being of all creatures.

When we look at the challenges that the earth is facing, we know that while we each have a responsibility to respond to the issues of climate change and environmental degradation, we cannot solve these on our own. In fact, our participation in the global economy contributes to the escalating crisis that our planet faces. We are used to buying food, clothes, and other products that damage the environment, rely on cheap (and often exploitative) labor costs, and require massive transportation (leaving a significant carbon footprint). We need to individually examine our practices.

Changing our individual choices, however, will not fix the problems our planet is facing. Nor can the church as communities of individuals solve our planet's environmental crisis. Instead, congregations invite us to join a movement that challenges the dominant practices of consumption that are prevalent in our society. Congregations cooperate with one another and join with community and environmental organizations in order to practice eco-centered ways of living that increase our care for the earth. Our willingness to work with others on issues of creation care acknowledges our interrelatedness with one another and all of creation. To address the challenges that lie before us requires trust and cooperation to seek a common good by caring for the earth. We will flourish as humans to the extent that our actions enhance the health of all creation.

Our relationship with God and with one another prompts us to live as communities that lean into the promises of God's redemptive work in creation. Rasmussen suggests that the church's role is to serve as an "anticipatory community," as those who live in a way that respects life for all creation. We give witness by living in harmony with the earth. In these acts, we hold open a new future for others to see. Rasmussen describes this in terms of a community's "prophetic symbols and practices," which prompt people to accept change and live into new possibilities. [10] As we recover a vision of the interconnectedness of the universe, the Spirit will animate us to work for the earth's healing. Our commitment to Christian vocation as part of our baptismal calling helps each of us to identify the particular gifts that we bring for service and to discover ways in which we can live out a vocation that demonstrates respect for one another and for all of God's creation. In this vision of life shared, we respond to God's call with a commitment to seek the good of all creation as we work for the health and well-being of all creatures.

ENGENDERING HOPE

While the challenges that we face are significant, the church brings a sense of hope to the task of responding to the environmental crises and our call to care for creation. Our hope is grounded not in our own capacity to solve the problems we have created. Instead, our hope is in God's promise to redeem our world. The testimony of faithful people who have gone before us reminds us of God's faithfulness. The history of the Hebrew people's exodus from slavery in the land of Egypt provides hope that God will move within us and among us to lead us from bondage to new life. The story of Israel returning from captivity to reclaim and renew the land shows the stubborn persistence of people of faith in the face of enormous obstacles. The Gospel message of Jesus's resurrection following his death at the hands of the powerful testifies to God's ability to bring forth life in the midst of death. The emergence of the church from a small group of weary and discouraged disciples exemplifies the Spirit's life-giving presence.

Even though the church arrives late in responding to the environmental crisis and in answering our call to care for and honor creation, we come with a particular word of hope that the One who created heaven and earth will breathe new life into our planet. In this season of urgency, we bring with us a hope for the renewal of the earth as our home. Our prayers are not to escape this place for another, but that our prayers and petitions to God will lead us to care for all life on our planet. Thus, while the news of the planet's crisis is daunting, as people of faith we hold up hope that with God's blessing, we will find ways to work for the earth's healing. In this fragile space, we acknowledge the damage that we as humans have done to the ecosystem. We confess the ways that our actions contribute to harming the earth, and we vow to change our actions and live more responsibly as part of God's creation. We place our trust in the One who brings the gift of resurrection to guide us as we work for the earth's renewal.

As Christians join with others to care for the earth, we hold up hope for the journey ahead. We bring with us songs of praise for the goodness of creation and cries of lament for the earth's plight. Our sacred stories remind us of countless times when new life emerges from the ashes of despair. Our bodies carry the marks of our rituals that unite us with Christ and God's redemptive presence in the world.[11]

These are the gifts that the church brings to the table. We have much to offer and much to learn from those who have worked for decades to sound a warning about the planet's plight. Together, we can work for the changes that are needed. As we lighten our impact on the earth, we create a bit more room for the biodiversity that sustains life on the planet. As we learn to live within limits that respect the earth's needs, we experience a deeper connection to our environment. In these acts, hope emerges among us as a promise and blessing.

THE EARTH AS SACRAMENT

On our faith journey, the earth serves as both source and sign of ways to live in harmony. We bring with us hope and commitment to work for the earth's renewal as we learn to pay closer attention to the rhythms of nature and recognize our own place in this vast ecosystem.

On a sunny, summer day, Jan and I drove to Mt. Rainier National Park to visit the Grove of the Patriarchs, a forest of old-growth trees. We took a short hike back through the woods and crossed over the Ohanapecosh River. We found signs leading us into the forest, where thousand-year-old trees rise up out of the earth and tower more than 200 feet into the air. Magnificent cedar trees gently sway as the breeze blows through the woods. Mighty Douglas fir trees proudly stand their ground. Sturdy western hemlocks add color and texture to the forest's palate. A quiet sense of peace permeates the area.

I craned my neck upward to see the tops of the trees. As I stood there gazing toward the sky, my perspective of my place in the universe took on a different dimension. Next to these massive trees, I was small, and my years on earth were fleeting. These trees had witnessed hundreds of years of change. Storms, fires, volcanoes, glaciers, and humans all had their impact on the landscape. Through all the crises and change, the forest remained a home and habitat for diverse life forms, from the plants that grew on the forest floor to the animals and birds that made their homes in the woods. Even when humans found this sacred place and began to take from the forest for their own needs, these ancient trees stood tall, pointing toward the sky.

When the trees do fall, they lie in the forest for decades. As the trunks gradually decay, green shoots sprout from the aged and dying tree trunks. Small animals, bugs, and insects create homes within the trees strewn across the forest floor. New life emerges as the forest shows the timeless truths of the universe. Resurrection takes root in the midst of death. The testimony of the trees offers us a portrait of hope at this crucial moment in human existence. Finding our place in the universe involves listening to the earth's cries and its rhythm of death and life.

I opened this book by lamenting how human consumption led to the death of trees on the Greek peninsula, and I am closing by describing nature's ways of responding when there is adequate time and space for healing to occur. The earth is in crisis, and human consumption and the destruction of natural resources must lessen in order for the earth's rhythms and heartbeat to regulate themselves. The transition from an ego-centered to an eco-centered system requires us to change our perspective and our actions. Christian faith offers us guidance for the journey. When we relinquish the need to place ourselves and our needs at the center of the universe, then God's presence in the world and in our lives comes into clearer focus. We discover ourselves dwarfed by the mysterious universe, just as we do when we stand next to the towering fir tree. Yet, there remains an important place for us within this sensitive ecosystem. Our actions ripple through the landscape affecting life for all. In the grand scheme of things we may be small, yet our impact on the earth is massive. At the same time, the opportunity and responsibility to participate in caring for the earth offers us the chance to embrace our place in the universe and to revel in the beauty and diversity of creation.

As people of faith, we share a story about God's longing for us to experience salvation, a sense of wholeness when we join in God's redemptive work. As Christians, we gather around the gift of water to baptize those who join us in professing our faith in "God, the Father, almighty, maker of heaven and earth." Here, on this earth that God created, we discover and celebrate the Spirit's presence among us. Around a table set with bread and wine, we remember the story of Christ, the One who lived among us to show us and teach us the ways of God.

As Christians, we face a choice, then, on how to move forward in this time of dramatic change. Our anxiety over our shrinking membership rolls and receding place among the power brokers of society are signs of our fixation with our own ego needs. Moving from an ego-centered to an eco-centered approach in our congregations requires us to reevaluate our priorities. The Gospel invites us to give our lives away in the hope and belief that God will bring us new life. Will we spend our time mourning for the good old days, when we placed ourselves at the center of culture and exerted our power and rights? Will we fight to reclaim our position and sense of privilege? Is the only alternative to these ego-centered actions to give up and slowly but gradually die, leaving behind us only vestiges of the past: church buildings now reclaimed as restaurants and apartments in an increasingly secular society?

There is another way through this turbulent passage. By holding on to the signs of life in Word and Sacrament and in the Spirit's presence in one another and in the world around us, we discover step-by-step a way into a new future. Guided by Scripture's witness to the centrality of the earth, refreshed by the baptismal water that runs down our foreheads, nourished by the gifts of bread and wine that sustain us, surrounded by a community of believers who share these practices, sustained by the presence of the Spirit in us and among us, we nurture and care for this sacred earth in which God's presence is known to us.

On this journey, we are empowered by the divine love that permeates the universe. So let us take our place by sharing this love as we care for one another and for the earth. The words of the Russian novelist Fyodor Dostoyevsky offer us guidance for the days to come:

> Love all of God's creation, the whole of it and every grain of sand. Love every leaf, every ray of God's light! Love the animals, love the plants, love everything. If you love everything, you will perceive the divine mystery in things. Once you perceive it, you will begin to comprehend it better every day. And you will come at last to love the whole world with an all-embracing love. [12]

Loving the earth is a way of loving God: the earth as God's creation, the earth as an incarnation of Christ's body, the earth as a birthing place where the Spirit brings new life. The earth is God's gift to us, a sacrament in which we experience the divine presence woven into creation. The earth as sacrament laments death, yet rejoices in the gift of new life. The earth as sacrament celebrates when we share the gifts of God with the people of God as a way to tell the story of God's love affair with this world that God created. The earth as sacrament and as our home welcomes and invites us to build communities that encourage, nurture, and support the gift of life.

With God's help, we can do this. We can walk hand in hand, day by day, listening for the divine heartbeat throughout the universe and trusting in God's faithful presence to call, confront, correct, forgive, sustain, and guide us.

Liturgical Resources

ORDINARY TIME

Call to Worship

The heavens declare the glory of God.
The firmament proclaims God's handiwork.
The plants and trees show God's presence.
Let us join with creation in praising God.

Prayer of the Day

God of all creation, who moves and inspires us through every time and season,
We bless you and praise you for the gift of life in your good created world.
Grant to us grace and humility to so order our lives

that we may honor you among all peoples and nations,

create wholesome and right companionship with our fellow living creatures,

and work for the healing of this world that you created.
Teach us to see and hear your power in the winds and waves, mountains and valleys, and rivers,
so that we may glorify your goodness to us and live rightly in your creation.
We pray to you through Jesus Christ our Lord, who lives and reigns with You and the Spirit,

Three in One, One in Three, now and forever.
Amen.

Confession and Pardon

All creation invites us to join our voices in praise to God. Trusting in God's mercy and grace, let us confess our sin to God and one another.

Generous God, you created us and placed us here to care for all of creation.
Forgive us for turning away from you and for neglecting the earth.
Raise us up and make us again stewards of your creation that we may see your presence in all that surrounds us; through Christ we pray. Amen.

Hear this good news to all who long to see and encounter Christ.
Today, salvation comes to this house.
Know that we are forgiven, and live in peace with one another and with the earth.

Prayer for Illumination

Shine your light on us, God, as we gather around your word. By your Spirit, make our lives fertile ground in which your word takes root and grows, through Christ we pray. Amen.

Prayer of Dedication

Bless these gifts and our lives, O God, that we may share ourselves and our belongings with those in need. Lift up our voices with those of all creation that sing out in praise for your grace and love. Amen.

ORDINARY TIME EUCHARIST

Scripture: Meal images from Luke 19 (Zacchaeus)

Invitation to the Table

Jesus invites us to hurry and come to the table.
Here, in this bread and wine, may we encounter Christ who
Calls us to care for the poor, the earth, and all who are in need.
All who long for Christ are welcome at this table.

The Lord be with you.
And also with you.
Lift up your hearts.
We lift them up to the Lord.
Let us give thanks to God.
It is good to give our thanks and praise.

God of creation, you created life and declared it good.
When we turned away from you and exploited the earth, you sent prophets to call us back to your way.
When we searched for you, you continued to call us through creation, prophets, and signs of your presence in the world around us.
In Jesus Christ, you call us to follow you and to work for the healing of the nations.
So we praise your name with sycamore trees and all creation as it sings:

Holy, holy, holy Lord,
God of power and might.
Heaven and earth are full of your glory.
Hosanna in the highest.
Blessed is the one who comes in the name of the Lord.
Hosanna in the highest.

We praise you for Jesus, who searches out sinners like us
And who breaks bread with all who hunger for new life.
In his baptism, teaching, healing, dying, and rising,
we encounter your redeeming presence.

* * *

Receive us and these gifts of bread and cup that we share today that they
May bring salvation and wholeness to our lives.

Great is the mystery of faith:
Christ has died.
Christ is risen.

Christ will come again.

Pour out your Spirit on us
and these gifts of bread and wine
that we make from the wheat and grapes that grow on this earth.
As we encounter Christ in bread, cup, neighbor and creation,
May we turn from our selfishness
and share what we have with the poor.
Give us strength to work for the day when all the world will live in harmony,
Through Christ who seeks us out and restores us to life. Amen.

Lord's Prayer
Breaking of the Bread

Hurry and come down,
    For today, Christ meets us at this table.
    Today, salvation comes to this house.
    These are the gifts of God for the people of God.

Notes

PREFACE

1. Paul Galbreath, *Leading through the Water* (Lanham, MD: Rowman & Littlefield, 2011); and Paul Galbreath, *Leading from the Table* (Lanham, MD: Rowman & Littlefield, 2008).

2. The triduum stands at the center of the church year with the celebration of Maundy Thursday, Good Friday, and the Easter Vigil as the first celebration of Easter.

3. For more on the catechumenate, see Galbreath, *Leading through the Water,* chapter 2.

4. For a fuller exploration of the shape of Eucharistic prayer, see Galbreath, *Leading from the Table.*

1. RECONNECTING TO THE EARTH

1. For example, Christian ethicist James K. A. Smith describes the way that bodies acquire habits through participation in rituals and practices in worship. While I disagree with his conclusion that gives preferential treatment to selected Christian narratives, Smith raises important questions about the priority that is often given to strictly intellectual approaches to faith. See James K. A. Smith, *Imagining the Kingdom* (Grand Rapids, MI: Baker Books, 2013).

2. See Michael Budde, *The Borders of Baptism: Identities, Allegiances, and the Church* (Eugene, OR: Wipf and Stock Publishers, 2011).

3. For example, note how a lack of inclusive language reinforces gender roles and stereotypes. Hierarchical patterns of power and privilege reinforce a perspective of human (especially male) domination that assumes the right to exploit the earth for humanity's own benefit. Reformed theologian Belden Lane portrays the human desire to possess all that is around us as leading us to "patriarchical, racist, and anthropocentric attitudes of dominion toward the 'other.'" Belden C. Lane, *Ravished by Beauty: The Surprising Legacy of Reformed Spirituality* (Oxford: Oxford University Press, 2011), 40. To what extent, then, does an exclusive use of male, patriarchal language endorse this approach?

4. Lane, *Ravished by Beauty,* 36.

5. "On the Care of Creation," Evangelical Environmental Network, http://www. creationcare.org/blank.php?id=39.

6. For example, in 1972, John Cobb published *Is It Too Late? A Theology of Ecology.* In the 1970s, the World Council of Churches began initiatives on justice and ecological sustainability that culminated at the 1983 assembly in Vancouver in calling member churches to make a commitment to justice, peace, and the integrity of creation. Other voices have called for the church to become active in environmental discussions, but the church as a whole has been slow to respond to those calling us to take action.

7. Most mainline denominations have offices that advocate for environmental justice. Many of these offices now provide some worship resources. Other nonprofit agencies offer a wide range of materials and services for congregations to use. I have used resources from Earth Ministry in Seattle and am impressed by their work with congregations to build awareness of ways to care for creation. See http://earthministry.org.

8. See the work of the Advent Project, especially the list of papers that link the project to justice and creation concerns at http://www.theadventproject.org/Documents/apsscholarships-up.pdf.

9. Norman C. Habel, David M. Rhoads, and H. Paul Santmire, *The Season of Creation: A Preaching Commentary* (Minneapolis, MN: Fortress Press, 2011).

10. "Celebrating the Season of Creation gives us a vision of what that kind of worship could be like every liturgical season—as we celebrate the role of Christ in redeeming creation and the work of the Holy Spirit in sustaining creation." Habel, Rhoads, and Santmire, *The Season of Creation,* 20.

11. Habel, Rhoads, and Santmire, *The Season of Creation,* 37.

12. Liturgical scholar Gail Ramshaw referred to this tendency to view nature as "nice" in her presentation at the Societas Liturgica Congress in Würzburg, Germany in summer 2013. Ramshaw's current work in writing Eucharistic prayers seeks to provide a more holistic approach to nature or, as she puts it, "less interested in sunsets than in the food chain." For a copy of her Earth Eucharistic Prayer, write to her at gailramshaw@verizon.net.

2. SEEING OUR PLACE IN THE WORLD

1. George Bowering, "Cascadia," in *Cascadia: The Elusive Utopia,* ed. Douglas Todd (Vancouver, BC: Ronsdale Press, 2008), 266.

2. I should note that in some ways the Native American church incorporated elements and images from Native American spirituality, while at the same time insisting on a Christian identity distinct from traditional Native American spiritual practices and articulating a theological perspective aligned with the far right of the denomination.

3. Samuel Torvend, "The Failure and Promise of Liturgical Orientation toward Care for This Wounded Earth," Societas Liturgica presentation, Würzburg, Germany, August 2013.

4. Dietrich Bonhoeffer in Larry Rasmussen, *Earth-honoring Faith: Religious Ethics in a New Key,* 84. "Only when one loves life and the earth so much that with it everything seems to be lost and at its end may one believe in the resurrection of the dead and a new world." See also Dietrich Bonhoeffer, *Dietrich Bonhoeffer Works,* Volume 8: *Letters and Papers from Prison,* ed. John W. de Gruchy; trans. Isabel Best, Lisa E. Dahill, Reinhard Krauss, and Nancy Lukens (Minneapolis, MN: Fortress, 2010), 213.

5. Rasmussen, *Earth-honoring Faith,* 111.

6. James K.A. Smith, *Imagining the Kingdom,* 36. Italics in original, words in brackets added.

7. Imagination is a creative way in which liturgy helps us see and experience the world around us from a different perspective. See Smith, 126. "Liturgical animals are imaginative animals who live off the stuff of the imagination: stories, pictures, images, and metaphors are the poetry of our embodied existence."

8. See David Power, *Sacrament: The Language of God's Giving* (New York: The Crossroads Publishing Company, 1999), 173. Power notes that imagination is not simply a matter of our own intellectual cleverness, but an openness to the work of the Holy Spirit. "To open the sacramental imagination, whether to other cultures or to the post-modern, communities have to

learn by experience to forego that kind of representational imagery which tries to bring the past or the divine into immediate presence, by the power of institution, the power of ritual imitation or the power of conceptual thought and locution."

9. http://www.pcusa.org/research/panel/summaries/panelsacraments02-09summary.pdf.

10. Cláudio Carvalhaes, "'Gimme de kneebone bent': Liturgics, Dance, Resistance and a Hermeneutics of the Knees," *Studies in World Christianity* 14, no. 1 (April 2008): 2.

11. Carvalhaes, "'Gimme de kneebone bent'," 16.

12. Ludwig Wittgenstein, *Zettel*, trans. G. E. M. Anscombe (Berkeley: University of California Press, 1967), Z461, 82e.

3. MEALS, VALUES, AND THE EARTH

1. See http://www.webofcreation.org/earth-bible.

The basic aims of the Earth Bible Project are to

1. develop ecojustice principles appropriate to an earth hermeneutic for interpreting the Bible and for promoting justice and healing of Earth;
2. publish these interpretations as contributions to the current debate on ecology, ecoethics and ecotheology;
3. provide a responsible forum within which the suppressed voice of Earth may be heard and impulses for healing Earth may be generated.

2. Larry Rasmussen, *Earth-honoring Faith: Religious Ethics in a New Key*, 147.

3. Rasmussen, *Earth-honoring Faith*, 147.

4. Rasmussen, *Earth-honoring Faith*, 148. "*Oikos* is, then, a knowledge and vision of economics, ecology, and ecumenics as interrelated dimensions of the same world."

5. See Paul Galbreath, *Leading from the Table* for my analysis of 1 Corinthians 11. Paul is addressing the malpractice in the church at Corinth by admonishing the community that the Lord's Supper requires equal sharing of food and wine with all who are present. Notice that Paul's instructions parallel the practices of the early Christian community in Acts 2, which provided for any in need.

6. Paul Bradshaw, *Eucharistic Origins* (Oxford: Oxford University Press, 2004), vi.

7. Bradshaw, *Eucharistic Origins*, 59.

8. Andrea Bieler and Luise Schottroff, *The Eucharist: Bread, Bodies, and Resurrection* (Minneapolis, MN: Fortress Press, 2007), 115. It is worth noting that the passing of a rule does not necessarily mean that all communities immediately followed it.

9. Dennis Smith, *From Symposium to Eucharist: The Banquet in the Early Christian World* (Minneapolis, MN: Fortress Press, 2003) 89. "Thus any group that sought to maintain its group identity tended to model itself on the clubs. Consequently, both Christian and Jewish groups were often taken to be equivalent to religious clubs by the ancients."

10. Dennis Smith and Hal Taussig published a brief examination of their thesis in *Many Tables: The Eucharist in the New Testament and Liturgy Today* (Norwich, UK: SCM Press, 1990). Since that time, they have separately published major works on the influence of Greco-Roman meals on the development of early Eucharistic practice. See Dennis Smith, *From Symposium to Eucharist: The Banquet in the Early Christian World* (Minneapolis, MN: Fortress Press, 2003); and Hal Taussig, *In the Beginning Was the Meal: Social Experimentation and Early Christian Identity* (Minneapolis, MN: Fortress Press, 2009).

11. Matthias Klinghardt, "A Typology of the Communal Meal," in *Meals in the Early Christian World: Social Formation, Experimentation, and Conflict at the Table*, Dennis E. Smith and Hal Taussig, ed. (New York: Palgrave Macmillan, 2012), 14.

12. Klinghardt, "A Typology of the Communal Meal," 14.

13.   In commenting on Paul's depiction of meal practices in Corinth, Dennis Smith notes, "Social bonding at the meal provided the experiential component, and likely even the generative matrix for Paul's theology of community." Smith claims that Paul's theological understanding of community grew out of his own experiences of sharing Christian meals. See Smith, "The Greco-Roman Banquet as a Social Institution," in *Meals in the Early Christian World,* 28.

14.   Dennis Smith, "The Greco-Roman Banquet as a Social Institution" in *Meals in the Early Christian World.* Dennis E. Smith and Hal Taussig, ed. (New York: Palgrave Macmillan, 2012), 30.

15.   Smith, 30.

16.   William McDonough and Michael Braungart, *Cradle to Cradle* (New York: North Point Press, 2002), 150. I am indebted to Marisa Mangum for pointing out these interesting parallels.

17.   McDonough and Braungart, *Cradle to Cradle,* 171–73.

18.   John 21 extends this portrait as Jesus connects love to the work of feeding his sheep. Here, shared values are focused toward a particular end of caring for others.

4. A BAPTISMAL WAY OF LIFE

1.   For further exploration of these themes, see Paul Galbreath, *Leading through the Water.*

2.   Careful readers will note that while the people of ancient Israel wandered in the wilderness for forty years before crossing the Jordan River, Jesus's entry into the Jordan River precedes his forty days in the wilderness.

3.   In fact, I wonder if the adaptation of Greco-Roman meal practices may have provided a model for adapting ritual cleansing practices.

4.   Immersion in a *mikveh* pool was both a ritual for those converting to Judaism as well as an ongoing cleansing practice for Jewish men and women.

5.   Bryan D. Spinks, *Early and Medieval Rituals and Theologies of Baptism: From the New Testament to the Council of Trent* (Aldershot, UK: Ashgate, 2006), 35–36.

6.   Spinks, *Early and Medieval Rituals,* 12.

7.   "The Didache," VII, translated by Cyril Richardson in *Sacraments and Worship: The Sources of Christian Theology,* ed. Maxwell E. Johnson (Louisville, KY: Westminster/John Knox Press, 2012), 107.

8.   Linda Gibler, *From the Beginning to Baptism: Scientific and Sacred Stories of Water, Oil, and Fire* (Collegeville, MN: Liturgical Press, 2010), 24.

9.   Gibler, *From the Beginning to Baptism,* 8.

10.   Melito of Sardis in Gibler, 22.

11.   John Hart, *Sacramental Commons: Christian Ecological Ethics* (Lanham, MD: Rowman & Littlefield 2008), 91. See also Galbreath, *Leading through the Water,* 113–18; and Rebecca Barnes, "Polluting Our Baptismal Waters," http://www.presbyterianmission.org/ministries/today/Polluting-our-baptismal-waters-0613/.

12.   Gibler, *From the Beginning to Baptism,* 32. Gibler notes that when less water was used in baptism, the church began to rely on lengthy prayers of blessing the water (as if it weren't already sacred). She brilliantly concludes: "Water is now a metaphor for what it was once known to be in itself."

13.   See Galbreath, *Leading through the Water,* chapter 2, for more on the ancient roots of the catechumenate.

14.   "Liturgy for the Reaffirmation of Baptismal Vows," Joint Commission on Doctrine from the Church of Scotland and the Roman Catholic Church in Scotland, 2010, 6. http://www.churchofscotland.org.uk/__data/assets/pdf_file/0011/3116/baptism_liturgy.pdf. The conveners of the Joint Commission write in the document's foreword that the entire liturgy "is gladly offered for use beyond the bounds of the two denominations on any ecumenical occasion when it is appropriate to recall and reaffirm our baptism" (page ii).

15.   Larry Rasmussen, "Eco-Justice: Church and Community Together," in *Earth Habitat,* ed. Dieter Hessel and Larry Rasmussen (Minneapolis, MN: Fortress Press, 2001), 18.

16. See particularly their Green Congregation starting suggestions.

17. Larry Rasmussen, *Earth-honoring Faith : Religious Ethics in a New Key*, 121.

18. Rasmussen, 227.

19. Presbyterian Church, "Commissioning to Ministry Outside a Congregation," in *Book of Occasional Services* (Louisville, KY: Geneva Press, 1999), 130. Language for commissioning those who serve both within and outside a congregation is identical.

20. This action challenges the normative pattern of allowing only ministers and particular church leaders (such as elders and deacons) to participate in the act of laying on of hands during ordination services. By ordaining congregational members to serve as Earth Stewards, we recognize that our baptismal callings require all of us to participate in care for creation. A similar logic suggests that the ordination of ministers (as well as elders and deacons) is grounded in our baptismal vows and welcomes the blessings of all who participate in this ritual act.

5. PRAYING WITH THE EARTH

1. Dianne Everson, musician and artist extraordinaire, created this fantastic piece.

2. Linda Gibler, pp. 38–40.

3. *The Prayers of Saint Francis,* compiled by W. Bader (New York: New City Press, 1988), p. 42.

4. *The Prayers of Saint Francis*, 42.

5. It is important to keep one central place of baptismal water clearly identified.

6. Reginald Zottoli, http://www.uua.org/documents/zottolireginald/flowercommunion. pdf . My thanks to Carol Alice for describing this service to me.

7. Alice Berry, in Zottoli, p. 2.

8. Zottoli, p. 3.

9. I am grateful to Claudio Carvalhaes for leading this service.

10. Rosemary is not mentioned explicitly in the Bible, but its prevalence in the Middle East prompts many readers to conclude that general references to herbs likely included rosemary.

11. Human consumption sometimes compounds these occurrences by accelerating the earth's natural cycles.

12. I am indebted to Chip Andrus for this suggestion.

13. Some communities have a tradition of not having a prayer of confession during the season of Easter. This prayer of thanksgiving takes the place of the confession and pardon during the Easter season.

6. WORSHIP BEYOND THE WALLS

1. Larry Rasmussen, *Earth-honoring Faith: Religious Ethics in a New Key*, 198.

2. Rasmussen, *Earth-honoring Faith*, 199.

3. Rasmussen, *Earth-honoring Faith*, 199–200.

4. "Shavuot," *Wikipedia*, http://en.wikipedia.org/wiki/Shavuot.

5. Julie Barnes, "Ministry in Nature: A Vision Realized," San Francisco Theological Seminary, http://sfts.edu/news/view_event.asp?ID=319 .

6. I am indebted to Presbyterian pastor Laura Mendenhall for this suggestion.

7. Philip Newell, *Celtic Benediction: Morning and Night Prayer* (Grand Rapids, MI: Eerdmans Publishing Co., 2000).

8. "How the Easter Date Is Determined," timeanddate.com, http://www.timeanddate.com/calendar/determining-easter-date.html. Orthodox Christians calculate this differently, which leads to different dates for celebrating Easter.

9. Joseph Renville, *Presbyterian Hymnal* (Louisville, KY: Westminster John Knox Press, 1990), #271.

10. Wendell Berry, *The Unsettling of America: Culture and Agriculture* (San Francisco: Sierra Club Books, 1977), 14.

11. I have adapted this liturgy that was originally prepared by my student Beth Olker.

7. THE EARTH AS HOME

1. Hymn text by Arthur E. Brumley. *Hymns of Faith* (Carol Stream, IL: Hope Publishing, 1980), 311

2. Dieter Hessel, "The Church Ecologically Reformed," in *Earth Habitat: Eco-Injustice and the Church's Response,* ed. Dieter Hessel and Larry Rasmussen (Minneapolis, MN: Fortress Press, 2001), 203.

3. Thomas Berry, *The Great Work: Our Way into the Future* (New York: Bell Tower, 1999), 391–92.

4. H. Paul Santmire, *Ritualizing Nature: Renewing Christian Liturgy in a Time of Crisis* (Minneapolis, MN: Fortress Press, 2008), 24.

5. Santmire, *Ritualizing Nature,* 8.

6. Larry Rasmussen, "Eco-Justice: Church and Community Together," in *Earth Habitat,* ed. Hessel and Rasmussen, 7.

7. Santmire, *Ritualizing Nature,* 25.

8. Dietrich Bonhoeffer, *Dietrich Bonhoeffer Works,* Volume 4, *Discipleship,* ed. Geffrey B. Delley and John D. Godsey, trans. Barbara Green and Reinhard Krauss (Minneapolis, MN: Augsburg Fortress Press, 2001), 226–30.

9. Michael Parsons, "'In Christ' in Paul," *Vox Evangelica* 18 (1988), 27–28.

10. Bonhoeffer, *Dietrich Bonhoeffer Works,* Volume 4, *Discipleship,* 225, footnote 2, "The present situation in church and theology can be summed up in the following question: Does the church take up a space in the world, and if so, what kind of space is it?"

11. Larry Rasmussen urges people of faith to recognize that to live "in the disciplined ways of sacramentalism, mysticism, asceticism, prophetic-liberative practices, and wisdom, are the spirited lifeways that renew and recast human responsibility." Larry Rasmussen, *Earth-honoring Faith: Religious Ethics in a New Key,* 361. Rasmussen explores each of these characteristics that constitute "religious ethics in a new key" that will lead to the transformative work of creating an earth-honoring faith (Rasmussen, *Earth-honoring Faith,* 111).

12. Fyodor Dostoyevsky, *The Brothers Karamazov* (Chicago, IL: Encyclopedia Britannica, Inc. 1952), 167.